ALL ABOUT
Spangle
Budgerigars

by
Roy Stringer
and
Fred Wright

First Published 1994
Copyright © 1994
Roy Stringer and Fred Wright

All rights reserved. No part of this book may be reproduced or transmitted in any form or by any means, electronic or mechanical, including photocopying, recording or any information storage and retrieval system, without permission in writing from the publisher.

ISBN 0 9518145 5 9

Typeset in New Century Schoolbook and Printed in Britain by Spottiswoode Ballantyne, Colchester, Essex, England. Published by Roy Stringer Publications, Somerdale Cottage, Station Road, Westbury, Shropshire.

CONTENTS

Acknowledgements 5

Foreword by Eric Peake 7

John Scoble introduces Spangles 11

Harry Bryan looks back 14

Meet the Experts 16

Chapter 1 Their Birdrooms 20

Chapter 2 Management 28

Chapter 3 Feeding 35

Chapter 4 Medication 40

Chapter 5 Their Studs 57

Chapter 6 All About Spangles 61

Chapter 7 Colour Expectations 84

Acknowledgements

Roy Stringer and Fred Wright gratefully acknowledge the kindness of Eric Peake in offering us the idea for this series of books and for painting the lovely Spangle Budgerigar on the cover, the great effort put in by Les Lockey, himself a very successful champion breeder, exhibitor and judge of Budgerigars, in travelling around Britain to take photographs of the experts, their birdrooms and – most importantly – their superb Spangle Budgerigars specifically for this book (unfortunately, Jeff Attwood unavoidably had to cancel the photo-session with Les Lockey but Mick Freakley was able to make good the omission at the last minute – and Reinhard Molkentin's move from Germany to South Africa reduced the opportunities to acquire photographs), Harry Bryan, for delving into his wonderful memory to recall some outstanding Blues from the past, Brian Byles, Editor of *Cage & Aviary Birds* and Peter Moss, Editor of *Bird keeper* for their support and advice during the book's preparation. Special thanks to Major Graham Macdonald (retd) – a Scottish gentleman and Budgerigar breeder living in Germany – for translating Reinhard Molkentin's contribution. Then, of course, there are the experts who have answered dozens of questions in our quest to discover what it is that has brought them success at the highest levels with Spangle Budgerigars; Jeff Attwood, Vic Smith, Bill & Chris Heale and Reinhard Molkentin. We thank them all.

The objective of the authors* of this book – and the other books in the *All about* . . . series is to offer a platform for some of the world's most successful breeders of particular Budgerigar varieties to reveal their techniques, methods, likes, dislikes and hopes for the future. We believe we have succeeded. The experts have not been "led" when answering the comprehensive range of questions put to them and editing has been kept to the minimum required. After studying their answers, readers might like to look for the reasons behind each expert's success.

You will not find the colour standards or scale of points of any organisation in this book – for more than one reason. Different countries have different standards. There is a distinct possibility that an international standard could be agreed before the end of the century. If you want to read a particular club's standards you can join the club – the space in this book is better devoted to the opinions of the breeders who have proved their ability by winning at the very highest levels. Colour standards and points allocations vary from country to country, but an outstanding Budgerigar is recognised the world over.

(Roy Stringer, formerly a design engineer in the motor industry, is Features Editor of CAGE & AVIARY BIRDS. Fred Wright, once a teacher, is now a freelance avicultural consultant to several companies and a regular contributor of articles to CAGE & AVIARY BIRDS and other avicultural magazines. Both are successful champion breeders and exhibitors of Budgerigars and international judges.)

FOREWORD
by Eric Peake

It was in the late 1970s that I heard the exciting news that a new mutation of Budgerigar – the Spangle – had appeared in New Zealand, and then in Australia. Leading Australian Budgerigar expert, John Scoble, was close to the situation as he explains in his introduction to this book. I find his theory that there is a link between Recessive Pieds and Spangles particularly interesting.

I find it amazing that another mutation – the Clearbody, which originated in the USA – shows similar characteristics to the Spangle, particularly when young. On close observation, the flights and tails of both Spangles and Clearbodies show a reversal of the normal colour pattern, ie: white with black edging in the Blue series and yellow with black edging in the Green series. A most distinctive feature of early Spangles was their "bulls-eye" mask spots; a dark outer spot with a clear inner area. But the feature from which the Spangle derives its name are the shell feathers (the semi-circular feathers) on the wing which extend from the area of the secondary flights right up to the wing butt.

Breeding Budgerigars for more than 40 years has given me a solid foundation of knowledge, but it is my artistic eye that enables me to "see" differences of feather composition and character. The factors that make a Spangle's wing feather different to a Normal's are, perhaps, more obvious to a trained eye.

For some years after the appearance of the Spangle there was much talk about "Spangle wing feathers being edged with black". Examination of the painting of the Spangle Dark Green on the cover of this book shows that this is just not true. The fact is that the black on the wing feathers is in the same position as on a Normal, but is narrower. It is the absence of grey coloration from these feathers that gives them – and Spangles – their distinctive appearance.

Early Spangles displayed particularly intense body colour and they certainly combined very well with Dark-factor birds; Cobalts, Mauves, Violets, Dark Greens and Olives. Even today, when some of the early features have been, at best, neglected and, at worst, lost, a Violet Spangle is one of the most beautiful Budgerigars around. Add the Yellowface factor and you create a Budgerigar of real brilliance.

A feature of the first Spangles, which was soon noted and put to use, was their fertility; exceptional when compared with the established varieties. They also had a fantastic capability for increasing in exhibition quality and size in the space of just a few generations. Because of this, they were paired with every available mutation. This was in spite of the pleading of Alf Ormerod (who brought some of the first Spangles into the UK) to pair

Spangles only with Normals. Almost certainly because of being crossed with the established mutations, their fertility and rate of improvement have levelled off as the years have passed

Normal Spangles
The characteristic Spangle markings are displayed to best effect on Normals, including the clarity of the reversed tail and flight patterns. Had Spangles been paired only with Normals right from the start, I am sure that they would be far better marked today than they are. Depth of body colour is another important feature of Normal Spangles.

Double-factor Spangles
Another striking feature of the Spangle factor is that when it is carried in double-dose – to produce a Double-factor Spangle – a Budgerigar is produced that does not resemble the Single-factor form that I have been discussing up until now. The Double-factor Spangle has been described as a clear yellow or a clear white Budgerigar. Although that description is true of some Double-factor Spangles, the majority carry a certain amount of body colour; often displayed as a bib below the mask. Some carry so much body colour that there is a definite contrast with their wings, making them look like faded Clearwings. It is difficult to see how anyone can set a standard for a variety that is so diverse in its appearance.

Perhaps because I spend so much time painting birds, their appearance makes a great impression on me and, on this basis, I do not see Double-factor Spangles as being Spangles at all, no matter what their genetic make-up. For me a Spangle must have the distinctive Spangle markings. When it comes to showing, I believe that Double-factor Spangles should not be exhibited in the Spangle class. Judging, like painting, is based on what you can see, not what the pedigree book shows.

Opaline Spangles
The continuous crossing of Opalines with Spangles has caused a lack of definition and blurring of the characteristic markings on Opaline Spangles. As a consequence, there is a wide variation of markings to be seen in Opaline Spangles today. Patchiness of body colour, particularly around the neck area, is also apparent. A true Opaline Spangle should display intense body colour, opalescent wing markings and a clear white or yellow head.

Other Variety Spangles
Due to their incredible fertility and their original ability to increase size, Spangles have been paired with many other varieties in the hope that they will transmit these qualities, particularly to "lesser" varieties. The result is that, in many cases, the typical Spangle markings have all but disappeared.

For example, when the Spangle factor is combined with Clearwing undesirable (from the Clearwing standpoint) clear tails begin to appear and cheek patches are broken and vary in colour. When Spangle is combined with Recessive Pied the wing markings (an important feature of Recessive Pieds) become blurred.

Finally, some breeders are under the impression that they can breed split Spangles, but this is an impossibility. As a dominant, the Spangle mutation shows itself when only one of its factors is present. Having said that, an interesting aspect of the Spangle is that it has been proved that non-Spangles bred from Spangles are particularly useful for producing good Spangles. It is my sincere hope that breeders will concentrate on Normal Spangles in an effort to return to the beauty of the original variety.

INTRODUCING SPANGLES
by John Scoble

■ *Like several other Budgerigar mutations, the Spangle first appeared in Australia, so who better to reflect on the past and future of this beautiful variety than Australian expert John Scoble.*

In my view, much misleading information has been published about the origins of the Spangle Budgerigar – even to the extent of the parents being identified. I am certain we will never know how and when the first Spangle was bred as, almost certainly, the person who bred it did not realise it was a new mutation. According to the late Frank Gardner, a Budgerigar breeder of high repute, Mr Jones of Victoria was the first to recognise they were something new and managed to acquire a number of them.

After a period of colony breeding they came to the notice of the Budgerigar Council of Australia. This was in 1977. The first time Spangles were seen by the general public was when they were exhibited in Melbourne. Although Frank Gardner advised Mr Jones to hang on to them, he was presented with a pair of Spangles. Thus, Frank Gardner became the first exhibition fancier to breed with Spangles.

Frank's record-keeping was very precise, extending to such details as cheek patch colour and mask spot configuration and so it may well be best not to pay too much attention to the word-of-mouth histories of the Spangle and to concentrate on what Frank Gardner's records have to tell us.

It is acknowledged by customs officials that large numbers of eggs of many varieties of birds are smuggled into Australia, every year. It is said that the first three Recessive Pieds entered Australia from continental Europe in this manner in the early 1970s – a couple of years before the first Spangle appeared.

The link between radioactivity and mutations is well recorded and this prompted me to follow up a particular line of investigation. Airline luggage passes through X-ray checks and, in addition, there was a radiation scare over Victoria around the same time. I checked with a poultry research centre and was told that the level of radiation, in the circumstances described, could not be responsible for the mutation of the Spangle.

It was explained to me that – although mutations of plants are caused deliberately under strictly controlled conditions – it would take a higher level of radiation occurring at a specific moment in an embryo's development to have caused a Recessive Pied to mutate to a Spangle. As far as I was concerned this put an end to this line of thought. Even so, I consider it strange that the Spangle mutation did not appear elsewhere in the world, as happened with other mutations.

Interbreeding Dutch Pieds with Recessive Pieds has demonstrated that grizzle markings, so characteristic of the Recessive Pied, can be transmitted to other Budgerigar varieties. Furthermore, A. Brown, of Sydney, bred the first Dark-eyed Clears in Australia from a Recessive Pied. For me, this strengthens the theory that Spangles could have mutated from Recessive Pieds, even if it was not as a result of the radiation sources previously identified.

The undersides of many Spangle feathers are grizzled, Spangles and Recessive Pieds both have broken cheek patches and early Spangle hens had much darker wings than their male counterparts – a feature shared only with the Recessive Pied. I possess Recessive Pied wing feathers that look very much like those taken from Spangles and clear head spots are common to both varieties.

Militating against the relevance of the head spot is the fact that this has been appearing on Budgerigars in Australia (New South Wales and Victoria) for 40 years. Such birds had been shown regularly in Victoria and birds marked like this often won Pied classes. Thirty years ago, I discussed the appearance of head spots on otherwise Normal birds with the man I rate as the greatest bird man I have ever known; Billy Hoare of Sydney. Mr Hoare maintained that they were a recessive form of Pied.

The Spangle mutation appears to be unique in that it has a factor which rearranges the pigmentation within the structure of the feather and, in addition, possesses a recessive modifier that acts as a diluting agent (to produce the Double-factor Spangle) when inherited from both parents. This is a phenomenon that exists in no other mutation. The first Double-factor Spangles bred by Frank Gardner had no ghost markings on their wings or body colour suffusion when in nest feather.

The whole question of coloration in Spangles is confusing because no two Spangles seem to be the same. In my experience, the markings of most single-factor Spangles reduce in density at every moult, while the opposite is true of double-factor Spangles, in which there can be intensification of wing markings (including under the wings) and body colour at each successive moult.

One of the tasks that needs to be tackled is finding how to maintain colour intensity on single-factor Spangles. It is frustrating when markings at the nest-feather stage approximate to the ideal, only to fade with time. I feel that successive single-factor to non-Spangle matings could be to blame for the loss of distinctive features such as the target-shaped spots and split-coloured cheek patches. In a lecture I presented at the 1985 Budgerigar Society Convention, I recommended using more Double-factor Spangles in pairings and experience has shown that this approach has produced better-marked single-factor Spangles.

Photographs of early Spangles in my possession show just what has been lost. They had brighter body coloration and distinctly marbled markings. Flights and tails had a dark edge which greatly improved the outline of the whole Budgerigar. This was demonstrated clearly in the course of experimental work that I carried out with wild Budgerigars, in conjunction with Neville Seage and Gary Heather of Sydney – whose contributions I rate as absolutely invaluable.

When a wild cock was paired with a Spangle hen the resultant Spangles displayed the beauty of the originals. Their spangling was superb, even though there was coarser feather and more down on the youngsters. Such results must encourage specialist breeders as they demonstrate what can be done – in practice, not theory.

Harry Bryan looks back

■ *Harry Bryan is the most successful Budgerigar fancier the world has ever known. He began keeping Budgerigars in 1916 and is still enjoying success on the show bench. In the intervening years he saw all of the top Budgerigars in the UK which until recently, in Budgerigar terms, meant the world. His memory is as keen as ever and here he recounts his memories of one of the most recent mutations, the Spangle.*

In the late 1970s I heard the news about one of the most exciting events in Budgerigars for the last 20 years. A new mutation, the Spangle, had been brought to Europe from Australia, by Rolf Christen. Top German fancier, Reinhard Molkentin (*featured in this book*) got hold of them, bred from them and let a few come to the Ormerod & Sadler partnership in the south of England.

I went to see Alf Ormerod and Doug Sadler and immediately fell in love with these vividly-coloured, beautifully-marked Budgerigars. After breeding with them for a season, Alf Ormerod let me have one of the original Spangles; a Cobalt cock that was quite small and not much of an exhibition bird. I believe that mine was the second stud in Britain to contain a Spangle. I paired the cock with one of my best Grey Green hens and produced six chicks, four of which were Spangles; two Cobalts and two Grey Greens. In compliance with the agreement I had made with Alf, I gave him two of the Spangles.

The following year, I paired the young Spangle Cobalt cock with another good Grey Green hen (which was carrying the Yellowface mutation) and bred the super young Spangle Yellowface Skyblue cock that was, at the age of only five months, the first of its variety to take the best breeder and best in show awards at a championship show. I also bred a hen of the same colour and some people thought she was better than the cock. She certainly had a beautiful back-line. The brother and sister were first and second in their class at the first Budgerigar World show.

The fertility of Spangles in those early days seemed to be 100 per cent. When you paired a Normal with a Spangle and the hen laid six eggs, you expected to get six chicks – and the proportion of Spangles seemed to be higher than the 50 per cent that the theoretical breeding expectation indicated. Spangles were paired with every other mutation in existence and now, less than 20 years later, they are no more fertile than any other variety and, if anything, I find that they produce less Spangles than the 50 per cent theoretical expectation.

The first breeders of exhibition Spangles were careful to pair them with only the best Normals in their studs. They recognised that pairing with diluting mutations, such as Cinnamon, Greywing, Opaline, Clearwing and

Dilute, would only serve to spoil the Spangle's unique markings. Since they became generally available, Spangles have dropped in quality, though one notable exception was the Spangle Grey Green cock that won so many prizes for the B & C Heale partnership (*also featured in this book*).

One of the special features of the Spangle is that when you pair two together, a proportion of the chicks are Double-factors; clear White or Yellow Budgerigars. To say that they are "clear" is not quite accurate. Many Double-factor Spangles carry signs of their body colour, mainly as a band below the mask. I don't like Double-factor Spangles. I don't see the point in them. The Spangle is essentially a bird of beautiful markings so there seems little purpose in breeding versions – be they Spangle Opaline Cinnamons, Spangle Whitewings, Spangle Yellows, Spangle Lutinos OR Double-factor Spangles – that have very few or no markings at all. If it was within my power to lay down the number of points that could be deducted from a Spangle that does not have distinct, well-defined markings, I would specify far more than the 25 currently allocated by the Budgerigar Society.

Spangles ought to be able to command a place in any stud of exhibition Budgerigars. I also believe we should be trying to restore the beauty of the Spangle that has been lost so quickly by indiscriminate pairings. Because they are dominant in their mode of inheritance it should not be too difficult a job. Introducing more Dark-factor Budgerigars – such as Dark Greens, Cobalts and Violets – would be a good start. My own Spangle Violet cock, that had already taken a best young bird in show award before being made best Spangle in show at the 1993 National Exhibition of Cage & Aviary Birds, was said to be a Budgerigar of beauty by many unbiased viewers. They are so new that there is not a great deal of history to the Spangle, but if you put your mind to it you could help to add to the story of the Spangle that fanciers of the future will be writing.

(*"The Budgerigar Man", the Harry Bryan story and way of breeding exhibition Budgerigars is available from the publishers of this book*)

MEET THE EXPERTS

JEFF ATTWOOD lives in the peaceful village of Stoke Gabriel, on the banks of the river Dart, in South Devon, England. It is in a tourist area and the temperature rarely drops below 45deg F (7deg C). In high summer, the temperature in his birdroom sometimes tops 100deg F (38deg C); in Jeff's view, an ideal place to breed Budgerigars. He has many overseas contacts and is a popular lecturer, about Budgerigars, all over the world. In 1965, Bill and Gladys Hellier came to see Jeff's Budgerigars, became firm friends and, in 1974, partners. Their Cinnamons (based on Mrs Moss and George Jenkins stock (which itself was based on Moss/Bryan bloodlines)) were legendary. In 1979, most of Attwood & Hellier's best birds were stolen and Jeff is convinced that this was a contributory factor to Bill's death, at the age of 59, just five years later. Since then Gladys and Jeff have continued the Budgerigar partnership. Although the Attwood & Hellier partnership has taken some of the top prizes on offer; best in shows and challenge certificates, Jeff now has a particular interest in new mutations and trying to re-establish, neglected, old varieties. He became aware of the Spangle mutation in the late 1970s and was eager to obtain a specimen. Spangles are now an important component of his stud and, at the time he made his contribution to this book, he was president of the Spangled Budgerigar Breeders' Association. In the course of experimental breeding he has combined many other mutations with Spangle.

VIC SMITH lives in a small village named Worrall, about five miles north of Sheffield, in the north of England. He joined the Budgerigar Society in 1954 and, for many years, enjoyed a great deal of success with his partner, the late Stan Wainwright. The Smith & Wainwright partnership was deservedly world famous. Over the years, Vic's name has been associated with various Budgerigar varieties, such as Cinnamons, Opaline Cinnamons and Recessive Pieds. He visits Harry Bryan every year and in 1983, although Harry had only six Spangles, he let Vic have a young Spangle Cobalt hen. Until then, there were only four people in Britain with Spangles; Harry Bryan, Alf Ormerod, Doug Sadler and Jeff Attwood. In December 1983, Vic organised a trip to the German AZ show and was so impressed by the Spangles on show that he bought two of the exhibits; Spangle cocks shown by his friend, Reinhard Molkentin. The Bryan Spangle Cobalt hen was paired with a Light Green cock and produced 16 chicks, including a Light Green Spangle cock that was fifth best champion breeder at the 1984 Budgerigar Society Club Show. This youngster brought Vic Smith the honour of being the breeder of the first Spangle to win a challenge certificate (CC) at the great event; for best Any Other Colour. In all, the Spangle Light Green cock took 12 challenge certificates and was best in show 12 times at almost every major show in Yorkshire. Vic Smith's greatest achievement came with an outstanding Grey Green cock, which was second best Budgerigar at the BS Club Show in 1991 and went one better to take the supreme award in 1992.

BILL and CHRIS HEALE live in Trowbridge, Wiltshire, in the south-west of England. Although they did not take up keeping Spangles until 1987 they have enjoyed outstanding success with the variety. It all happened by chance. Bill won a judging competition at a meeting of Bristol B&FBS and his prize was a young Spangle Opaline Grey Green cock, which had been donated by local champion exhibitors, Clifton and Marion Wixon. From such a fortuitous beginning, an outstanding Spangle family was built. The most successful Spangle this husband-and-wife partnership has bred to date, a Spangle Grey Green cock, has 24 challenge certificates (CCs) to his credit and is known affectionately as "Big Daddy". In 1989, the first time that CCs were put up for competition specifically for Spangles at the Budgerigar Society Club Show, it was Bill and Chris Heale who won the two on offer. Big Daddy took the any age CC and his son, another Spangle Grey, was awarded the breeder CC. Also in 1989, the adult was judged best Budgerigar in show at Swindon B&FBS and the youngster was best breeder in show at Bristol B&FBS; both championship events. Another Spangle Grey son of Big Daddy, from his second breeding year, was best Spangle breeder in show at the Specialist & Rare Variety Budgerigar show in 1990. This was bettered in 1991 when Big Daddy himself was best Spangle in show. The Spangles were still taking top awards in 1994; including best champion adult in show at Worcester BS championship show and best young Spangle awards at two championship events.

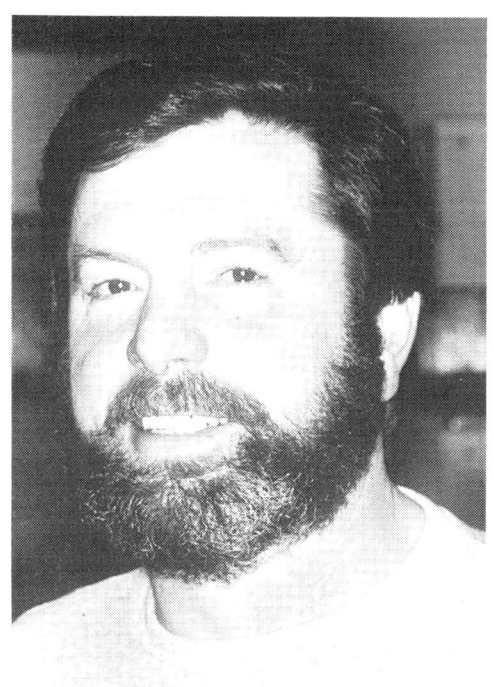

REINHARD MOLKENTIN is one of the best-known Budgerigar breeders that Europe has produced in the last 30 years and his name will always be linked with the Spangle mutation. In 1979 he was contacted, at his home in Karlsruhe, Germany, by his friend Rolf Christen, a Swiss who had gone to live in Australia. Rolf had imported the first Spangles into Europe and visited his parents' home in Switzerland regularly. The size of the Christen Spangle stud soon increased to around around 50. The quality of the Swiss-bred Spangles was better than the originals because Rolf Christen's Normals were from the Maurice Finey bloodline. He decided to sell the Spangle stud and approached Reinhard who bought the remaining 40 Budgerigars. The rest had gone to three fanciers; two Swiss and one German. Reinhard was quite aware that he possessed something special but resisted the temptation to breed from every Spangle, regardless of its quality. He used only the best 10 Spangles and paired them with the very best of his own stock, which meant top-quality, because he was the top breeder in Germany at the time. It was because Spangles were paired with such high-quality Normals that they improved so quickly. By 1985 he had bred 500 Spangles and was spreading the message to top Budgerigar breeders from all over the world, being one of the main lecturers at the Budgerigar Society's Diamond Jubilee Convention, in Birmingham. It was from Reinhard Molkentin that the first Spangles came to Britain. After having won top prizes in Germany for many years, Reinhard Molkentin went to live in South Africa in 1993.

CHAPTER 1

THEIR BIRDROOMS

Describe your birdroom.

Jeff Attwood:

The design of my present birdrooms did not come about by chance. The rooms are the result of 40 years' experience; starting from a small garden shed. Both rooms are made of timber on a brick surround. Both have concrete bases but the larger room has a timber floor set above the concrete. The roofs are slightly sloping and covered with bitumen felt. The main room contains inside flights and stock cages and is used primarily as a stock room, for the training of young birds and the preparation of sales and show birds. Occasionally, some of the stock cages are used for breeding. It measures 30ft x 12ft x 11ft (9.1m x 3.6m x 3.3m) at its highest point; just within the building control limits. There are 18 stock cages (three rows of six) on the back wall and the removal of slides can create three 18ft (5.5m) long flight cages. There are storage cupboards beneath. On the opposite wall is a stainless steel sink unit, with hot and cold water laid on, large storage cupboards and 12 stock cages above. Down the centre of the room is a box with a hinged lid, containing six seed bins. Suspended above this is a 9ft (2.7m) long stock cage; 3ft wide by 2ft high (91cm x 61cm). The inside flights measure 12ft x 6ft x 9ft (3.6m x 1.8m x 2.7m) high and are sited at both ends of the room. They lead to two outside flights measuring 20ft x 12ft (6.1m x 3.6m) and 12ft x 12ft (3.6m x 3.6m). All except the centre of the roofs of the outside fights are covered to protect them from the droppings of wild birds. The small open area permits the birds to enjoy the benefits of rain. In the floor of the flights are drains which lead to the mains drainage. This means that I can hose down the floors and the water runs right away. I believe that Budgerigars benefit from large flights where they can build up muscle rather than fat. Budgerigars are made to fly, so I let them! I learnt in Australia that Budgerigars are brought into breeding condition by rain so I have installed a mains-supplied, battery-operated, computerised, misting system in the flights. It operates three time a day and the Budgerigars come outside as soon as it starts. The second room is used only for breeding, and measures 14ft x 10ft x 9ft (4.3m x 3.0m x 2.7m) at its highest. I believe that ventilation is essential, even in winter. Indeed, I believe that dead-in-shell can be caused just as much by a build up of moisture as a lack of humidity. Ventilators and windows are set above the cages, so that every part of every wall – except where the door is – can be used for cages. Ventilator bricks in the lower walls ensure a through-flow of air. The 45 breeding cages are of all-wire construction and measure 24ins long x 17in square (61cm x 43cm x

There are 45 all-wire cages in Jeff Attwood's breeding room. He describes it as being like a colony system.

Outside Jeff Attwood's breeding room where he uses the all-wire cages.

43cm). The access door and nest-box are at one end. I have used this design since 1979 and it has proved to be very successful. All of the birds can see each other (almost like a colony system) and there is plenty of fresh air circulating. There is a stainless steel sink unit, with hot and cold water, a storage cupboard and a winnower. The breeding room contains the electrical controls for both rooms. The seed for this room is stored below the cages in buckets fitted with covers. I use two types of nest-box; plastic and timber. I have always changed wooden nest-boxes every two years in case a build up of organisms might persist from season to season. I even wondered whether this might have something to do with French moult. I saw plastic nest-boxes in a novice's birdroom but felt that the white plastic they were made from might make it too light inside the box. I ordered 100 in black plastic, measuring 8in long x 8in deep x 5in wide (20cm x 20cm x 13cm). The timber concave is changed for each round, with fresh sawdust. They are mounted externally because I have found that inspecting internal nest-boxes disturbs the birds too much. The timber boxes are used in the overspill room and are large at 9in long x 10in deep x 8in wide (23cm x 25cm x 20cm). They were designed by Bob Travniceck, an American friend and fancier. I have to report that both types of boxes are equally successful. Deep nest-boxes are more important when all-wire cages are used. A chick which leaves the nest too early is far more comfortable on the floor of a conventional cage, among the seed husks and sawdust, than on bare wires. I use 1kw wall-mounted fan heaters to keep the temperature above 50°F (10°C). If the fancier is comfortable, the conditions are good for breeding Budgerigars. Fluorescent lights are controlled by time switches (with no false twilight) and there are two nightlights in each room. During the breeding season the main lights come on from 7am until 9.30am and from 4pm until 10pm. I may consider upgrading the lighting controls in the future. A water filtration system is installed, in which the filter needs changing only every five years. I did have an automatic watering system but it used to get furred up and needed to be drained regularly. I now use rabbit drinkers, with a small ball at the end of a tube. The birds soon found out how they worked and they are safe against contamination. *Vent-axia* have recommended an air-filtration unit which takes out 80 per cent of dust from the air. It consists of a filter which clamps onto a conventional extractor fan, positioned at ceiling level. The filter can be removed to be cleaned outside the room. An automatic humidifier operates when natural humidity drops below 75 per cent relative humidity. A *Rolex* incubator is used to give breathing space while trying to find an alternative nest for eggs that have been abandoned. Tea trolleys are used to wheel around seed, water, softfood and grit.

Vic Smith:

I have two birdrooms; one 24ft x 10ft (7.3m x 3.0m), the other 14ft x 8ft (4.3m x 2.4m). The larger room is 8ft (2.4m) high at the front sloping to 6ft-6in (2.0m) at the back. The smaller room has an apex roof. Both are

Outside view of Vic Smith's breeding room.

Vic Smith's stock room and flight.

constructed of timber, with thick wooden floors. The rooms stand on railway sleepers so that plenty of air circulates beneath them. The smaller room is equipped with six breeding cages, each measuring 30in long x 20in deep x 18in high (76cm x 51cm x 46cm), and two inside flights which lead to two outside flights, each measuring 12ft x 6ft (3.7m x 1.8m). I believe this to be the ideal size for outside flights. If they are longer, the Budgerigars in them become so lean that it can be difficult to put weight on birds when you bring them in to prepare them for showing. Budgerigars also become very flighty in large flights and so are difficult to train for the show cage. The larger room has no inside flights but is equipped with a block of 24 breeding cages of the same proportions as those in the smaller room. My external nest-boxes have been in use for more than 30 years. They are 9in long x 6in wide x 9in (23cm x 15cm x 23cm) deep and fitted with a wooden concave and stepping block. The larger room has hot and cold running water and its lighting is totally automatic, being controlled by a timer, dimmer and an over-ride sensor that puts the lights on if the sky becomes dark during the day. Tubular heaters are controlled by thermostats to maintain the minimum temperature at 45°F (7°C). Two ionisers help to keep the air fresh. The smaller room has similar equipment except that it has only one ioniser and no running water.

Inside view of Vic Smith's breeding room.

Describe your birdroom:

Bill and Chris Heale:

Our birdroom is of breeze-block construction and measures 24ft x 8ft x 8ft-6in high (7.3m x 2.4m x 2.6m). The walls have been rendered, inside and out. The inside walls are painted with white, washable emulsion

Bill and Chris Heale's birdroom.

Breeding units constructed of melamine-faced chipboard in Bill and Chris Heale's birdroom.

and the outside treated with stone paint and sealer. The slightly-sloping roof, of corrugated asbestos, is insulated and fitted with a rooflight. Light also enters through aluminium-framed windows in the walls and ventilation is increased by airbricks. The room is in two sections and there are two entrance doors, both fitted with safety doors. No outside flights are used. When we had them they were underused in hot weather and the noise they generated when it was very windy was enough to cause hens to leave nests of fertile eggs. We extended the room so that it could contain two large inside flights. These can be used independently, to house cocks and hens separately, or can be connected through a bobhole. The flights have been positioned so that breeding pairs can see into them and the sight of other Budgerigars acts as a breeding stimulus. We have 23 breeding cages, arranged around the rooms in blocks of 16, three, two and two. The larger block is made from melamine-faced chipboard and has individual cages which measure 18in x 12in (46cm x 30cm), but the removal of dividers creates four 6ft (1.8m) long stock cages. The block of three cages and one of the blocks of two have individual units measuring 30in x 15in (76cm x 38cm). The remaining two cages measure 18in x 15in (46cm x 38cm). In addition, there is a large stock cage which is used to house youngsters when they are taken away from their parents. Each breeding cage is equipped with two square-sectioned perches (to give the hen a better grip when being mated) and an open-topped wooden box into which go all of the food dishes. The cage floors are covered with wood shavings obtained from a safe source. Small wooden dishes fit to the back wall of the cage to hold grit and a peg supports cuttlefish bone. A small wooden table is placed in the corner of each cage to provide shelter for any chicks that might be attacked by their parents. Our nest-boxes are external, made from compressed wood fibre and fitted with removable concaves. They measure only 6in x 6in (15cm x 15cm) in section as, in our view, in larger boxes eggs and chicks can become chilled. Each box has a sliding inspection door at the front, beneath which is a large lower lip to contain chicks and eggs. On the cage side of the box there is an entrance hole and perch. Sterilised, softwood shavings are placed in the boxes. Our overall set-up is conventional with a few extra gadgets. Lighting is provided by two fluorescent tubes in each section. A timer controls the tubes in section one – used only in the show season. The nightlights are blue tungsten bulbs; 15 or 25 watt. There is an extractor fan, an ioniser and a radio in each section. Heating is provided by an economic heater in section one and a tubular heater in section two. The aim is to keep the temperature to at least 45°F (7°C), both for our own good and the birds'. Two cages are equipped with airing cupboard heaters so that they can be used as hospital cages. Wire mesh separates birds from the heaters. We choose to control lights manually. So much can go wrong in a birdroom and if you are there first thing in the morning and last thing at night you can take corrective action.

Reinhard Molkentin:

At the time of answering these questions, I had not yet set up my birdroom in South Africa, so the answers I give apply to my setup in Karlsruhe, Germany. My breeding room measures 28ft x 18ft (8.5m x 5.5m) and is located in the ground floor of my dwelling house. The walls are of stone and the floor is tiled. One of the 28ft (8.5m) long walls is equipped with wooden-framed, wall-to-wall windows. Ventilation is assisted by an electric fan, set at a height of 6ft-6in (2.0m) in the centre of the room. There is an inside flight, measuring 12ft-6in x 8ft (3.8m x 2.5m), and two outside flights, 9ft-9in long x 3ft-3in wide x 8ft high (3.0m x 1.0m x 2.5m). The perches run lengthwise to maximise the flying space. Within the breeding room, the cages are laid out in an "L"-shape. Along the length of the inside flight is a block of four cages, each the same size as a team show cage. These are very useful for training youngster to behave well when they are sent to shows. There are 44 breeding cages, each measuring 31in x 20in x 16in (80cm x 50cm x 40cm), and each equipped with one round and one square perch. The nest-boxes fit to the fronts of the cages and measure 10in x 10in x 6in (25cm x 25cm x 16cm). The nest-box design incorporates a box-within-a-box and so chicks and eggs are well controlled when the inner is removed to make inspections. The entrance hole, on the cage side of the box, is set very high to deter chicks from leaving the nest-box too early. The room has a supply of hot and cold running water and a main lighting system, supplemented by nightlights. A cupboard, to store spare seed pots, water vessels and perches; a food trolley; a vacuum cleaner and two ionisers complete the equipment.

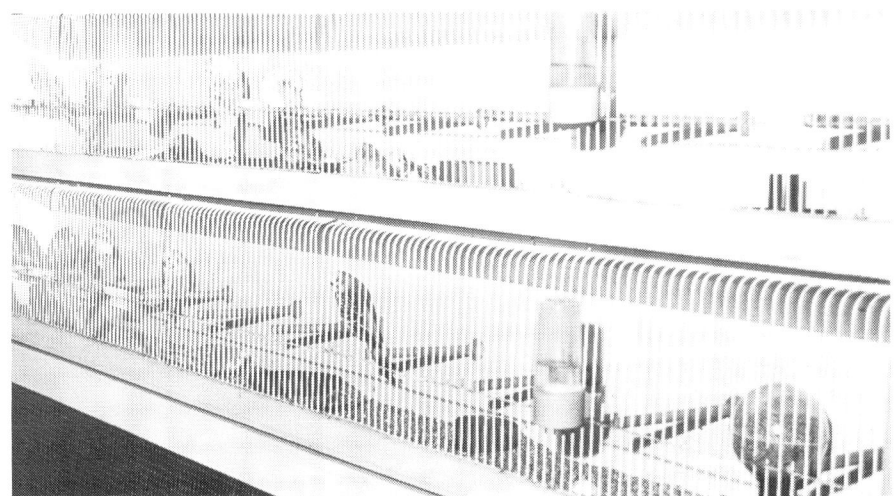

These training cages are used in Reinhard Molkentin's birdroom to steady young birds before they go into the flights.

CHAPTER 2

MANAGEMENT

Describe a typical day's activity in your birdroom during the breeding season:

Jeff Attwood:

My cocks and hens fly together throughout the year, until just before pairing. Then, selected cocks and hens are put in separate cages for three or four days. "Absence makes the heart grow fonder" and so they take to each other quickly when put in the breeding cages. I consider pair bonding to be very important, so the nest-box is not put on until the hen can be seen responding to the cock's advances. This makes fertility more likely. Once breeding starts, I try not to disturb the birds. The cages are checked for cleanliness every day, but before chicks hatch, nest-boxes are inspected only every two or three days. Once chicks hatch, daily inspections begin. Eggs are

Jeff Attwood uses both plastic and plywood nestboxes. Here a plywood box is attached to his breeding units.

handled as little as possible for fear of infecting them. Eggs are marked only when absolutely necessary. Wire cages tend to keep themselves clean because droppings fall through onto a sheet placed beneath. It takes me only 15 minutes to remove and clean the sheets of all the breeding cages. Extensive cleaning is only carried out between breeding rounds. The flights are cleaned out once a week. The walls of the inside flights are clad with *Laconite* (a plastic-faced board) and so are easily washed by spraying with disinfectant and washing with water. The perches are washed and the flight floors covered with thick brown paper. It is essential (especially in summer) to keep the outside flights clean. I have tried gravel, earth and grass floors, but concrete is definitely the best. The flight floors slope slightly so that water runs into the drains when I throw on two buckets of water containing bleach and then spray with a high-pressure hose. Good record-keeping is absolutely essential if you want to keep a close-knit stud of Budgerigars. In my birdroom, 50 per cent of what goes into the breeding cage comes out of the record book. I am looking into computerising my records, but I am not quite there yet so I continue to use a record book that I designed in 1974 and have supplied to many other breeders.

Vic Smith inspects nestboxes early in the morning when there are chicks about.

Vic Smith:

I visit both birdrooms every morning; at 7am on working days and a little later at week-ends. Only those nest-boxes that contain chicks are inspected during this visit – they are easily identified because they are marked with yellow labels. All cages are checked to make sure that their occupants do not need attention. This morning session takes about 20 minutes. The main work is done, to a strict routine, in the evening, starting at 6.30pm. Every nest-box is inspected, chicks ringed and breeding records kept up to date. The room is "hoovered". This, together with feeding and watering takes about 2 hours. All of Saturday morning is spent in the birdrooms. The rooms, flights and cages are given a good clean and feeders and drinkers are disinfected.

Bill and Chris Heale:

At between 7 and 7.30 am every morning, the lights and radios are switched on. Every pair that has chicks, or eggs due to hatch, receives bread and milk, in a coffee jar top, and *EMP*, in a finger drawer. The same pairs' nest-boxes are checked and the floors are swept. At around 10am, nest-boxes are checked again and half a millet spray is given to each pair. Chicks that have recently been taken from their parents are checked closely – making sure that they know where the drinker is. Over the years we have noticed that chicks that have not taken water take on a slit-eyed appearance. Chicks on breeding cage floors are checked to ensure that they have not been attacked. The health of the parents themselves is checked. Once chicks are a week old the nest-box is cleaned, every two days. All of this activity helps to increase our birds' confidence, which must help those who go to shows. The room is visited again at 3pm, when the flights are checked and a close eye is kept on hens, particularly maidens, that are due to begin hatching. At around 6.30 to 7pm, the main feeding and watering is done, which takes between 1 and 1½ hours. Record cards are brought up to date with notes made of eggs laid, chicks hatched and ringed. Eggs are marked with a soft pencil and checked for fertility. Hens' copious droppings are removed every day. On Saturdays, the spilt seed is cleaned out from the wooden boxes (our chickens are terrific layers) and drinkers are thoroughly cleaned in a solution of *Vanodine V18*. Shavings are changed in nursery cages every week, in breeding cages every two weeks and in the flights every two or three weeks. The lino-covered floors are washed and disinfected every week and the ceilings and fittings are wiped down twice a week.

Reinhard Molkentin:

It takes about an hour, every morning, to go through the room with the vacuum cleaner and to replenish seed dishes and water drinkers. During the breeding season, the main work is carried out in the evening. This includes thorough nest-box checks and every pair being given sprouted naked oats and eggfood. Grit and calcium blocks are checked and, when available, chickweed is fed. Week-ends provide the opportunity to clean out the flights and to clean perches. Otherwise, no special time is set aside for doing certain tasks. Wherever possible, each job is done immediately it needs doing.

Describe the activity in you birdroom during the lead up to a show.

Jeff Attwood:

I try to get the breeding season finished in June and begin to select likely candidates for the show team at the end of that month and in early July. Eight weeks before the first show, their main feathers are checked. Broken tails and flights are gently removed – though only one main tail feather is taken out even if both are broken; in case they never regrow. Four weeks later, the potential team – anything from 30 to 50 birds – is put into 18ft (5.5m) long stock cages; cocks and hens together. Their diet is adjusted (as explained in chapter 3). As time passes, dividers are inserted to reduce the number in each group and limit their flying space so that by the last week there are six birds in each 3ft (91cm) long cage. My Budgerigars never receive show cage training. The only time they enter show cages is when they are sprayed (every day, not later than noon) and when they go to a show. The first spray – a real soaking – is with warm water but as the show approaches cold water, with a little *Johnson's Plumespray* added, is used. I have a onc gallon, *Black & Decker* battery-operated spray which works well. Condition improves rapidly with spraying so after a few weeks it is difficult to get the feathers wet; the water just runs off. Spraying is stopped two days before a show. Varieties, such as Albinos, Lutinos and Lacewings may need to be hand-washed. For this I use *Johnson's* baby shampoo, a soft pastry brush (to put on the shampoo), my grandfather's badger-hair shaving brush (to rinse it off) and then a light spray. My approach to trimming masks depends upon how densely-feathered they are. A few excess spots can be removed in one operation but a heavily-spotted specimen is trimmed over a week, seven or eight feathers at a time, finishing three days before the show. Blood on a show Budgerigar's head, the day before a show, need not stop it winning. By washing with cold water (warm water fixes the stain), and shampoo, rinsing (a pinch of kitchen salt in the rinsing water helps) and keeping the bird in a warm place to dry, I have won several best in show awards. It is worth taking a chance with a bird that has a pin feather on its head or a mask spot missing, but it is a waste of time to send out a Budgerigar which is heavily flecked or has major feathers missing. It is not fair to a Budgerigar to send it to a show unless it has a chance of going forward for a major award. Show cages need not be brand new, but they should have their paint work touched up and be clean. Avoid gloss paint on the inside as it disturbs some Budgerigars. A few millet sprays on the stock cage floor helps to make sure that they feed just prior to being caged. Cage labels are fixed and the cages are loaded into carrying boxes. I very much prefer an estate car for transporting Budgerigars. There is a risk of exhaust fumes getting into a boot, with fatal results. If you have a saloon, transport the bird on the back seat.

Vic Smith:

Adult members of the show team and their young bird counterparts are treated differently. Adults are caged up (eight to a 5ft (1.5m) long cage) only three weeks before a show. This is because they can put on too much weight very quickly. The birds are kept in groups according to how much weight they are carrying. Those with a tendency to be overweight receive a diet of plain seed; no Japanese millet or groats. Slimmer birds are put on a more-fattening diet. Young birds are housed under the same regime, but are caged for a couple of weeks longer. No soaked seed is given during the show preparation period because it tends to keep the birds' plumage "loose". Tight feathering is the order of the day when the shows are coming up. For the first three days of caging, the birds are given a heavy spraying with warm water to which a capful of baby shampoo has been added. After that, spraying takes place every other day, with cold water, up until four days before a show. No broken flight or tail feathers are removed, because there is

This spraying cage is used when Vic Smith sprays his Budgerigars.

always a possibility that they might not regrow. In the early 1960s, I removed a mask spot from an outstanding Cinnamon cock and it did not reappear until 12 months later. My attitude is that if a bird is not naturally ready, it is better to keep it at home.

Bill and Chris Heale:

As the show season approaches we keep our eyes open for any birds that are showing potential. Broken tails and flights are removed at least nine weeks before the first show, though only one tail feather is removed (in case it doesn't regrow) even if both are broken. The potential show team is brought in from the flights 4 or 5 weeks before the show. Cocks and hens are housed separately. The perches in the show-preparation cages (three of the 6ft long units) are set higher than usual so that birds on the floor cannot pull the tails of birds on the perches. When spraying (two or three at a time), we restrict the birds to one end of the stock cage after the food has been removed. The first spray (from a garden mini-spray) consists of hot water and two drops of baby shampoo. We then spray every two days with water and once a week with *Plumespray*. If a bird drops a mask spot we remove the

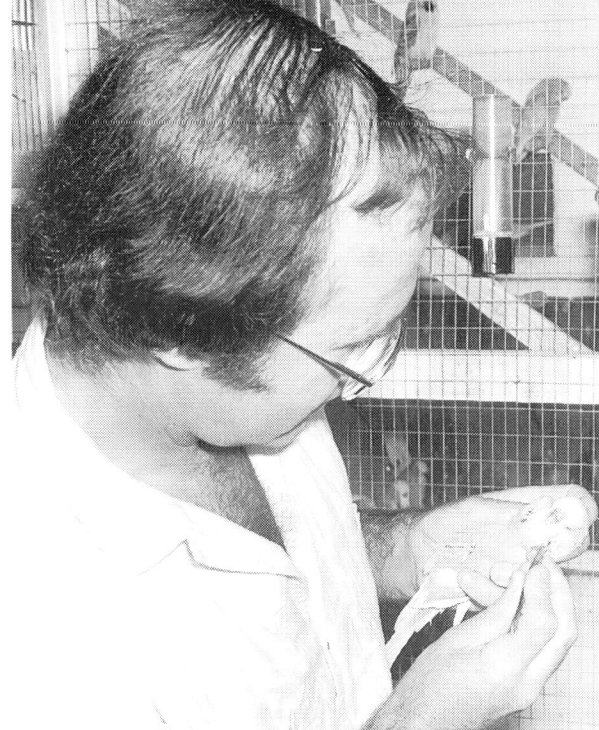

Bill Heale prepares the mask of one of his show team.

lot so that they grow in as a set. Show birds are kept on the standard diet with added dry groats – which are withdrawn if any sign of plumpness is seen. *Ascorbivite* (manufactured by *Vydex*) is added to the drinking water. Its extra vitamin C alleviates stress and keeps the birds in good condition. Show training consists of bringing birds in show cages into the house. For 30 minutes to an hour, we walk past them, do the vacuum cleaning, talk to them (they are fascinated by our three talking Budgies), get them used to judging sticks and visitors. We believe that this is much closer to the environment that show birds experience at a show, than a birdroom. Most of them settle down better when they are away from the aviary. When the birds are entered, we write the class numbers in a small notebook so that it is easy to check the labels when they arrive and when the birds are being put into the show cages. On the Monday, Tuesday and Wednesday before the show a light spray of *Plumespray* is administered. On Thursday excess mask spots, including shadow spots, are removed. On Friday, heads, especially above the cere, tails and flights are washed with warm water, baby shampoo and a toothbrush; rinsed and dabbed dry. On the night before the show, bent tails and flights are straightened in hot water – making sure that the birds are not scalded. Show cage perches are checked, both to see that they are firmly fixed and set at the specified height. Seed is put in the show cages. The morning of the show is the only occasion the lighting timer is used. The lights are set to come on one hour before we are due to leave home so that the birds have time to feed before being caged. Twenty-five minutes before we are due to leave, we go down to the birdroom with notebook and show cages. Once we are satisfied that all is correct, we place lightweight cotton covers over the show cages to prevent the occupants being disturbed – and set off to the show.

Reinhard Molkentin:

Preparation for showing begins eight weeks before the first show with birds being brought in from the flights to be housed in smaller, stock cages. The idea is to study them and to sort out which ones qualify to be in the show team. Every bird is handled and their feathers examined. Broken feathers are removed, firmly but gently, and masks are trimmed. The birds selected are washed and placed in the cages, with the cocks separated from the hens. In the eight weeks up to the show, between $1\frac{1}{2}$ to 2 hours is spent, every day, on the preparation of 20 to 30 Budgerigars. The birds with the best prospects are run through the show cages every day. They are spoken to and made accustomed to the judging stick. Every third day they are sprayed with cold water. Two weeks before the show the cocks are getting very fit – even frisky – and they are rehoused so that there are only two in any one cage. Three or four days before the show, masks are trimmed so that only the main six spots remain. For me, the most anxious time is not the show itself, but the time I actually put the birds in the show cages. By then, I have almost always known whether I would win or not.

CHAPTER 3

FEEDING

How do you feed your Budgerigars?

Jeff Attwood:

Basic seed mixture:
I find it surprising that some breeders pay large sums for birds and then feed them the cheapest seed. I have tried many seed suppliers and have not always been satisfied with the quality of some of their seeds. I look for a mixture containing good quality plain canary and a range of millets and for the past six years I have used *Trill*. It is ideal for my birds the whole year round. Some suppliers include seeds that sound good but if the birds don't eat them, they are a waste of money.

Extras:
Budgerigar tonic seed is fed two or three time a week, as a treat, with a handful of groats or small, whole oats added. I am a great believer in seeding grasses and, from April to September, my birds receive huge bundles every day. In the autumn, bunches of hazel twigs are offered and stripping the

Plastic seed hoppers are used in Jeff Attwood's flights.

bark helps to bring hens into breeding condition. When it comes to the breeding season it is unrealistic to expect exhibition Budgerigars to rear two or three rounds of chicks on plain seed alone, though my birds' diet is kept natural with no "commercial" vitamins. Naked oats (brand name *Denji* oats) are fed soaked. These are more nutritious than normal oats. My soaking set-up consists of two plastic buckets, one inside the other. The inner bucket has lots of small holes drilled in its bottom. The naked oats are placed in the inner and the buckets are topped up with water. After 12 hours the inner bucket is lifted out so that the water drains off. After a rinse the oats are left for another 12 hours before being fed. The basis of my evening softfood mixture is a "complete" dry dog food, put through a food processor to produce a granulated powder consistency. Well-washed carrots are grated and mixed in to produce a crumbly mixture. Grated carrot, alone, is also fed twice a week. In the mornings, wholemeal bread is damped with *Cow & Gate* baby milk. Wild greenfood – particularly chickweed, shepherd's purse and persicaria – is collected (taking care not to take from a field that has been sprayed). I also grow a form of beet, rich in iron, which I discovered while in New Zealand. Every pair with chicks receives half a millet spray every day. In the lead up to the show season, those birds that need to put on weight are fed a little extra Japanese millet, oats and the occasional millet spray.

Drinking water:
My birds' drinking water is filtered by the same system that we use in the house, so I know it makes it more palatable.

Additives:
Macrobiotics are coming into the Fancy and I brought some back from the United States where it is used with Parrots. It is said to make the digestion more efficient and brings the birds to maturity more quickly. After 12 months I have to say I see no difference, though this might be because my Budgerigars' diet is such that they need no more extras. In Australia, in 1990, I noticed breeders adding raspberry cordial to their birds' drinking water; 1 tablespoon to 2 pints (1.1l). I was told it contained the preservatives E122 and E123 (sodium metasulphate and sodium benzoate) and that these cleared out infection from a Budgerigar's gut. The only cordial I have found in the UK which contains both additives is a lime cordial marketed by the *Co-op*. I now use this all the year round and have no cases of droppings around the vent.

Grit and minerals:
There has been talk about Budgerigars not requiring grit. I believe they DO – and in variety. I collect grit from a beach near my home, in the early hours of the morning after there has been a high tide. It is given to the birds, still wet and without being washed, and they love it. I credit a lot of the fertility of my stud to the saltwater grit which has a high iodine content. I also give soluble grits such as oyster shell. *Caperns* is an excellent proprietary grit. Grit is offered in pots and strewed on the cage floors – a little and often. Since I kept Gouldian Finches, I always add a little medicated charcoal (for Pigeons) in

the dry grit mixture to clean the digestive system. A 2.2lb (1kg) bag of *Kilpatrick's* Pigeon minerals is also added to 28lbs (12.7kg) of grit.

Vic Smith:

Basic seed mixture:
As my basic seed mixture I use *Trill*; an excellent mix that keeps my birds fit.

Extras:
My Budgerigars relish small amounts of safflower, hemp and small sunflower seeds. *Maxifeed "B"* is given the whole year round and *EMP* (with added carrot and wholemeal bread which have both been put through a food blender) is given every evening during the breeding season. Soaked naked oats are fed morning and evening during the breeding season. Greenfood is never fed.

Drinking water:
Tap water is passed through a *Brita* filter jug to remove impurities. Drinking water is changed every day.

A mobile stock cage is used for young Budgerigars in Vic Smith's breeding room.

Additives:
Solvit, a multi-vitamin additive produced for the poultry industry, is added to the drinking water, at the rate of 1 teaspoonful to 8pts (4.5l) of water, for

six days a week. On the seventh day *Entrodex*, a probiotic supplied by *Vydex*, (highly recommended) takes its place.

Grit and minerals:
Mineralised grit and cuttlefish bone are always available. Grit pots are replenished every week-end. Pigeon minerals (pink and black) are always available in separate finger drawers.

Bill and Chris Heale:

Basic seed mixture:
We feed *Versele-Laga* No. 2 Budgie mix and *Versele-Laga* small Parrakeet mixture in separate dishes. We changed to this seed in 1992 after problems with another mix. The mixtures, together, offer a wide variety of seeds. They are also very clean.

Extras:
We give millet sprays occasionally to all birds throughout the year. We give damped *EMP* to the birds in the flights once a week to get them accustomed to it, prior to the breeding season. Greenfood is not offered because even the chickweed that grows in our own garden cannot be guaranteed against having been fouled by neighbours' cats. In any case, Budgerigars can gorge themselves on greenfood and their droppings become loose. Weaned chicks are given a little dry groats and millet sprays in addition to the basic seed mixtures. We do not soak groats or oats because they can go sour quite quickly.

Drinking water:
Drinking water comes straight from the tap – after it has been allowed to run for a few minutes to get rid of sediment. In winter months we take the chill off the water before giving it to the birds.

Additives:
We add *Ascorbivite* to the drinking water (5ml to 3pt (1.7l)) three times a week during the show season. The rest of the week we give plain water. *Vetreplex* (manufactured by *Vetrapharm*) is used every other day, starting a month before the breeding season at a dilution weaker than that recommended.

Grit and minerals:
We offer *Versele-Laga* mineralised grit. It contains a good mixture and is not too sharp. We use *Liverine* Pigeon blocks (containing salt and charcoal), cut into small chunks for the breeding cages and larger portions for the flights. Iodine nibbles are also used regularly. Cuttlefish bone is available in flights and cages.

Reinhard Molkentin:

Basic seed mixture:
My seed mixture consists of 40 per cent plain canary, 30 per cent white millet, 20 per cent Senegal or red millet and 10 per cent Japanese millet.

Extras:
Sprouted naked oats are fed daily and a good egg-based, softfood mixture is given to breeding pairs. In the warmer months, they get half-ripe seeding grasses and chickweed. Fresh willow is cut and hung up in the flights. Sunflower seeds, millet sprays and half-ripe maize corn are also fed in small amounts.

Drinking water:
Plain water is not given. In Germany many "teas" (infusions of herbs and fruit) are drunk and my Budgerigars receive the same fruit tea that I drink myself.

Additives:
Both young and old birds in the flights are given vitamin B every four weeks. Breeding pairs are not given extra vitamins because I believe that they upset their breeding rhythm.

Grit and minerals:
Grit and calcium blocks are always available. In addition, the cage floors are strewn with bird sand, which the birds enjoy picking over.

CHAPTER 4

MEDICATION

What do you look for when checking your birds' health and what do you do about it?

Jeff Attwood:

Generally speaking, if you manage your Budgerigars well, they will remain healthy. However, even when they are looked after very well, there are exceptions and so I check twice a day for any birds that are not looking well; signs such as being fluffed up, eyes closed, head over the shoulder, dirty vents and discharges from the beak. Leave a sick Budgerigar too long without treatment and you could lose it. Caught early, a little warmth clears up most minor illnesses within 48 hours. I have a plastic hospital cage, but I prefer putting a 75 watt dull-emitter lamp in front of a show cage. If I lose two or three birds in a short space of time (a very infrequent occurrence) I put all of the stock on a course of terramycin for three days, off for three days and back on for three days. It is important to complete the course. If one of my birds looks as though it is suffering from trichomniasis (head feathers matted with mucous deposits) I put it on a mixture of Emtryl soluble (1 pt (0.57l) of water with Emtryl added at the rate recommended on the packet) and terramycin (one teaspoonful). This is made fresh each day and given for seven days. Mites can occasionally attach themselves to Budgerigars, bringing such problems as scaly-face. Another form I have noted causes a skin eruption around the neck (usually on hens). A couple of applications of *Alugan* ointment usually solves mite problems. Eye infections (red and swollen or closed and watery) can be improved by one or two applications of chloromycetin eye ointment. Wounds, and even problems of feathers not growing properly, are treated with chlortetracyclin hydrochloride in powder form. I make great use of my local vet and for autopsies use the Ministry of Agriculture & Fisheries. Though each post-mortem examination costs £30, it is well worth it. New birds brought into a stud should be kept in cages separate from the rest for two or three weeks – or even better in a separate shed.

Vic Smith:

When you have kept Budgerigars for a long time, you can tell at a glance if a Budgerigar is unwell. A Budgerigar sitting quietly, fluffed up with a dull eye is the main warning sign. In my experience, if a bird showing such signs is put in a small cage on its own, with a heat lamp positioned in front, it is usually alright by the next morning. If a bird needs a quick supply of energy I give it glucose (glucose powder added to water) and *Complan* (a food made specially for convalescent humans) by way of a dosing tube, straight into the crop. I have saved more birds with warmth, glucose and *Complan* than any other method. Pure kaolin (sold as a medicine for children) is very useful when Budgerigars have stomach upsets.

Bill and Chris Heale:

We look for fluffed-up, lethargic birds that tend to sleep more often than the rest. A pumping tail is a bad sign – except when it is a hen that is due to lay. Green staining around the vent and head feathers soiled by mucous are indications that a bird needs treatment. We also look out for physical injuries, such as cuts. Any bird that does not look well is transferred to a hospital cage. Sick birds lose body heat quickly and so need to be kept warm if they are to stand a chance of survival. Birds with green vents or loose droppings are given cold, weak tea in their drinker. It is also administered straight into the beak with an eye dropper. If there is no improvement we consult our local vet, who is well-qualified with birds, and he prescribes antibiotics if they are required. If a bird has sour-smelling, fouled head feathers we put a pinch of Epsom salts into its drinking water and also administer some with a dropper, straight into the beak. With the relatively few birds we have had with this problem the treatment has worked. For cuts, we treat with witch hazel.

Reinhard Molkentin:

Thirty years of experience has taught me that it is very difficult to treat sick Budgerigars. It is better to prevent illness by keeping everything clean; cages, perches, feeding pots and drinkers. Cleanliness in the birdroom can avoid much sorrow. If a Budgerigar fluffs up its feathers or attracts attention by listlessness, it should be caught up so that its weight and vent can be examined. If the vent is dirty it should be cleaned with a mild disinfectant. Quite often, the only problem is that the bird concerned is going into a moult. If it is put into a cage on its own, where it can eat in peace, it will soon be alright again. Particularly with young birds, the gentle heat of an infra-red lamp help can speed recovery. For digestive problems I have a medicine called *Gabro-Col*, this is very effective against trichomoniasis.

What does your birdroom's medicine chest contain?

Jeff Attwood:

Terramycin, chloromycetin palmitate (given as a 50/50 solution in water, a bring-back-from-the-dead medicine), *Alugan*, aureomycin, chlortetracyclin hydrochloride, Emtryl soluble, chloromycetin eye ointment, *Collo-cal D,* eye dropper, crop tube, jeweller's sidecutter (for removing rings from swollen legs) and chloroform (to euthenase any terminally-sick bird). I now have a supply of a non-tetracyclin, synthetic, broad spectrum antibiotic named *Baytril* 5% solution. It is expensive but extremely effective when administered directly into the crop. *Baytril* is manufactured by *Bayer* of Suffolk and is obtainable from a vet.

Vic Smith:

A stainless-steel dosing tube, scissors, ring cutter, glucose powder, Complan, pure kaolin.

Bill and Chris Heale:

Optrex (for eye problems), witch hazel, *Ivomectin* (bird strength), *Ronidazole,* Epsom salts, *Vaseline,* ring cutters and chloroform water to put really sick birds humanely to sleep.

Reinhard Molkentin:

Gabro-Col, anti-flu paste, eye cream.

Do you use medication on a routine, preventative basis?

Jeff Attwood:

Although it is not medication as such, I give Budgerigars a combination of calcium and vitamin D (*Collo-cal D* from *C-Vet*) prior to the breeding season. Budgerigars need calcium to remain healthy and breed well. Vitamin D is needed to permit the absorption of calcium.

Vic Smith:

Medication is never given on a routine basis.

Bill and Chris Heale

We administer *Ronidazole* twice a year; in mid-May and a few weeks prior to the breeding season. We use this against trichomoniasis and believe it to be safer for Budgerigars than *Trykil.* Every bird is treated routinely against mite by putting a drop of the bird version of *Ivomectin* on the back of its neck; youngsters before they are first put in the flight and adults prior to the breeding season. Other medication (except those mentioned above) is given only on the advice of a vet. We have never wormed our Budgerigars.

Reinhard Molkentin:

I dispense medicine only when it is needed.

Vic Smith surveys the Budgerigars in his flight to be sure that all are well.

A hospital cage that is used in many birdrooms.

(above) Vic Smith's stockroom and flights.

(right) Inside Vic Smith's breeding room.
(photographs: Les Lockey)

(above) Bill and Chris Heale outside their birdroom.

The first Spangle challenge certificate winner for the B & C Heale partnership. (photographs: Les Lockey)

Yellowfaced Double-factor Spangle White hen – Reinhard Molkentin. (photograph: Reinhard Molkentin).

(left) Stock cages in Reinhard Molkentin's birdroom. (photograph: Theo Vins)

Double-factor Spangle Yellow cock – Jeff Attwood. (photograph: Mick Freakley)

Top quality exhibition Spangle Grey cock bred by Bill & Chris Heale. (photograph: Les Lockey)

A Spangle Skyblue cock from Vic Smith's collection. (photograph: Les Lockey)

(right) A young Opaline Spangle Grey Green hen bred by Les Lockey.

(left) Spangle Grey Green cock – Les Lockey. (photographs: Les Lockey)

Dark factor birds add much to the Spangle variety. This can be seen with Jeff Attwood's Spangle Dark Green cock. (photograph: Mick Freakley)

(left) The first Spangle in Germany to be bred by Reinhard Molkentin. (photograph: Reinhard Molkentin).

(right) Cinnamon Spangle Cobalt – Reinhard Molkentin. (photograph: Reinhard Molkentin).

A Spangle Grey cock bred by Vic Smith which shows good wing markings. (photograph: Les Lockey)

Spangle Grey hen from the B. & C. Heale stud. (photograph: Les Lockey)

(right) Cinnamon Spangle Grey cock – Vic Smith.

(left) Australian Yellow-face Spangle Cobalt cock – Vic Smith. (photographs: Les Lockey)

CHAPTER 5

THEIR STUDS

(Readers who are not conversant with the genetics of colour expectation will find it helpful to refer to Chapter 7 when the experts discuss pairings that produce Spangles).

How many Budgerigars do you keep and what varieties are they?

Jeff Attwood:

Glad Hellier and I have about 250 Budgerigars just prior to pairing. This number increases to around 600 by the end of the breeding season. Spangles (mostly Normal but including combinations with other mutations) make up about 10 per cent of the stud. We keep most of the popular varieties – Normals, Opalines, Cinnamons – plus more specialist forms such as Lutinos, Yellowfaces, Recessive Pieds, Clearbodies (which I was the first to import into the UK in 1989), Australian Goldenfaces (which I first imported in 1983) and a few Crested Budgerigars. I believe that panel judges should know about all varieties. I also feel a duty to preserve mutations for future generations. In the past, several were permitted to die out.

Vic Smith:

My stud normally consists of around 150 Budgerigars, of which about 30 are Spangles. The rest of the stud is made up mainly of Cinnamons, Opalines Cinnamons and Recessive Pieds.

Only a percentage of Spangles are kept in Vic Smith's stud of Budgerigars.

Bill and Chris Heale:

Just prior to the breeding season we have fewer than 100 Budgerigars; around 56 hens and 40 cocks. Of these, 15 are Spangles. By the end of the breeding season, according to how well it has gone, we would expect to have between 200 and 230 birds. We have had only one very poor breeding season to date and that was when we were second-year novices. That year we produced only 33 chicks. We keep a wide range of colours and varieties; Normals, Opalines, Dominant Pieds, Yellowfaces, Greywings, Cinnamons and Grey Yellows.

Reinhard Molkentin:

I keep about 150 Budgerigars from which to select my breeding team. I breed around 250 to 300 youngsters every year. About a third of my breeding stock is comprised of Spangles in nearly all of the colour varieties, including Double-factor Spangles, which I consider to be particularly valuable for breeding purposes. The rest of my Budgerigars are Normals, Cinnamons and a few Opalines. I have about 20 top-quality Saddlebacks. I used to have more, but reduced the stock by selling 60.

Which of the other varieties can improve your Spangles?

Jeff Attwood:

Spangles have developed into good exhibition Budgerigars so it is their markings that need attention. We have good Normals and these – particularly Dark-factors – are best for maintaining wing markings. I have found that the Normals bred from Spangle x Normal pairings can give wonderful wing markings. Introducing Australian Double-factor Goldenfaces into both my Blue series and Green Spangles has been very beneficial. They seem to add size and length of feather to Dark-factor Budgerigars and an Australian Double-factor Goldenface Spangle Violet is lovely to look at. Double-factor Spangle x Spangle has bred some well-marked Spangles for me. In spite of their being at a disadvantage on the show bench, Double-factor Spangles are worth keeping as stock birds.

Vic Smith:

At the present time there are far more Cinnamons in my stud than there are Normals. As a consequence, I am obliged to pair Cinnamons with Spangles. It must always be kept in mind that the overall quality of

Budgerigars is of supreme importance, regardless of whether it is a Spangle, a Normal or a Cinnamon. The close observer can see that a good, well-marked Spangle Cinnamon has the same shape and size of markings as a Normal Spangle and I find the delicate, dilution of the Spangle markings quite attractive. I cannot say the same of Spangle Opalines. The Opaline factor does not dilute a Spangle's markings, it destroys them. Having said all that, if I had a very strong stud of Normals, they would no doubt be my first choice of mates for my Spangles. However, theory is all very well. In practice, you have to use the best Budgerigars that are available to you.

Bill and Chris Heale:

Dark-factor Normals are particularly good for bringing out the best markings on Spangles. We have also found that when we pair Spangles with Normals that have come from Spangle x Normal pairings, the resultant Spangle progeny have particularly good wing markings and mask spots. Every three years we pair very good Opalines with some of the best of our Normal Spangles to help spot and overall size. The resulting Spangle youngsters are paired with good, clean Normals the following year.

This good young Grey cock is typical of the Normals that Bill & Chris Heale use to pair to their Spangles.

Reinhard Molkentin:

Between the years 1980 and 1984, I used the very best Normals and Cinnamons to develop Spangles to an extremely high level of quality. I was so successful that the situation is now reversed and I use Spangles to improve Normals!

A Yellow-face Spangle Cobalt bred by Reinhard Molkentin.

CHAPTER 6
ALL ABOUT SPANGLES

What is the attraction of Spangles and is specialising a good idea?
Jeff Attwood:

Even when enjoying a lot of success with Cinnamons, I was still interested in all other varieties. A good Recessive Pied is as pleasing to me as a good Grey Green. In the late 1970s I was excited to hear rumours of a new variety in Australia; the Spangle. Shortly afterwards, I heard that Spangles had reached Germany and rumours began to circulate about the high fertility and wonderful exhibition quality of the new mutation. Then, closer to home, Alf Ormerod (who always had close contact with German fanciers) acquired one. I did not see a Spangle until 1981, when Vic Smith (*also featured in this book*) persuaded Alf to release two Spangles; one for Mrs Angela Moss and one for me. My Spangle Grey Green cock was not a good exhibition specimen, but I was still thrilled, particularly in the knowledge that top-quality stock had been bred into the Spangles both by Reinhard Molkentin in Germany (*also featured in this book*) and Alf Ormerod. My confidence was justified. Paired with a good hen, the cock produced Spangle chicks that were much better than itself. The attraction of the Spangle was that it was entirely different to any Budgerigar I had seen before and, having a dominant mode of inheritance, had terrific potential for improvement. They reminded me of the descriptions of the early Opalines, I had heard given by Mrs Moss. It was not long before Reinhard Molkentin and I were exchanging birds. A big boost to my Spangle stock came when he swopped six of his high-quality Spangles for six of my Cinnamons and Opaline Cinnamons. What I did not realise, immediately, was that one of the Spangles (which looked like a very rich Grey Green) was an Australian Yellowface Grey; a wonderful addition to the stud. I do not think it is a good idea to specialise in Spangles. At Budgerigar Society 1990, I lectured on setting up a stud of Normal Light Greens, Afterwards, two great specialists (Arthur Snell with Greens and Derrick Bowley with Blues (*both of whom feature in this series of books*)) discussed with me the limitations specialists set for themselves. The restricted number of classes they can exhibit in – and the knowledge that a mixed stud can always throw up a single outstanding individual of their specialised colour. Specialising gives you more birds to choose from, when it comes to showing, but a lack of success could destroy your interest. Specialising is alright as long as you are winning!

Vic Smith:

I was attracted to Spangles when I first saw those that were in Harry Bryan's birdroom in 1983. I was thrilled when he let me have a young Spangle Cobalt hen. My enthusiasm for Spangles became even greater when, later that year, I saw them on the show bench at the German AZ show in Bremen. More than 10 years later, I am still attracted to Spangles, though I fear that the ones around today are far below the standard of those of the mid-1980s. In those early days, they were in the hands of only a few breeders, were considered to be something special and their mates were chosen very selectively. Fortunately, in the variety's infancy in Britain, they were owned by fanciers who had Budgerigars of the highest quality and who were prepared to use their best stock to breed more of these attractive Budgerigars. Today, Spangles are in nearly every aviary, the world over, and have been paired with every range of quality from best-in-shows to pets. Being paired with low-quality stock has taken its toll. I do not believe that full specialisation is an option that is open to the Spangle enthusiast. I could never contemplate a continuous programme of pairing Spangle with Spangle. Spangles fit well into most mixed studs, particularly those that are strong in Normals.

Bill and Chris Heale:

Even though we acquired our first Spangle by chance, they certainly have an attraction for us. When we were first married we kept Sebright "spangled" Bantams so it is a logical progression to keep Spangle Budgerigars. Having got off to a good start we are now faced with the challenge of maintaining and improving the quality of our very good Spangle family; making sure that they are well-marked and have the required bulls-eye spots. Although we do not specialise in any one variety we are very careful about the pairings for our Spangles. We line-breed to maintain their good points. It follows that we would not pair our Spangles into any variety that would dilute the wing markings of the progeny. Our main aim – throughout the whole stud – is to add gradually the various features that are needed to produce excellent exhibition and stock Budgerigars, in quantity. We admire fanciers who specialise because they keep certain varieties pure and, in some cases, keep them in existence.

Reinhard Molkentin:

I first saw Spangles when I visited, Rolf Christen, a Budgie friend in Switzerland. He had brought eight Spangles back from Australia and had paired them with Normals at his parents' home, near Basle. I was very surprised to see the attractive markings of this new mutation. Their diluted wings, completely novel mask spots and the full, deep body colour which contrasted so well with the wings, completely charmed me. The mask spots, with their clear inserts were unique. I bought Rolf Christen's complete stud. I put in a lot of work, crossing Spangles with my best Normals and within five years had expanded the variety virtually worldwide. At the end of that time I became a little bored with them and did not breed so many. However, since 1990 my interest has renewed and I work with many pairs. If you were able to keep 1,000 Budgerigars, there would be no problem in keeping lots of varieties and bringing all of them up to exhibition standard. As it is, no-one possesses unlimited space, so I think it is a good idea to specialise in a particular variety.

This baby Spangle Skyblue from Les Lockey's stud shows plenty of potential.

What makes a good – and a bad – Spangle?

Jeff Attwood:

A good Spangle is one that is a good Budgerigar and a true representative of the variety – and I fear that there are fewer now than there used to be. The position of the Spangle can be compared with that of the Clearwing. In Australia, Yellow-wings and Whitewings can be seen that have clear colour contrast between wings and bodies – particularly in Dark-factor birds. In the UK there are no longer Clearwings with the same contrast. In the early days, I saw Spangles that were so intense in colour that they shone like silver dollars. Every feather in their wings was distinctly outlined in black. If there are Spangles like that around today, I do not know where they are. There are plenty of badly-marked Spangles around and most of these are the result of being paired into other varieties, such as Opalines and Cinnamons. As long as national bodies do not allocate sufficient points for a Spangle's wing markings, we have a situation where judges have a ready-made excuse for putting up Spangles with insipid markings, if they are good Budgerigars in other respects. This does not help the variety.

Vic Smith:

Anyone who ever saw Harry Bryan's Yellowface Spangle cock (which was the first Spangle to take a best in show award at a championship show (Dorset B&FBS) and then went on to be best Spangle at the first Budgerigar World show), its Yellowface Spangle sister (which some observers thought was better than the cock) and my own Spangle Light Green cock (which did so much winning in the mid-1980s) knows what a good Spangle looks like. All three had size, shape, style and Spangle markings like they used to be. Sadly, there are very few around today that could match that trio. The features that make a Budgerigar "bad" are well-documented; narrow head, nipped-in neck, short mask, hinged tail, lack of size and the like. However, a Budgerigar that excels in good physical features can still be a bad Spangle by virtue of its marking faults. In my opinion, one of the biggest faults to be avoided are black markings (rather than the typical Spangle lacings) on the wings. Then there are the mask spots. Ninety-five per cent of all the Spangles I see have spots that do not comply with the "target" requirement. Many have no spots at all! I have yet to see an Opaline Spangle with good markings. The combination of the Opaline and Spangle mutations seems to create smudgy wing markings, reminiscent of the Opaline wing markings that were around before the standard was altered to call for normal wing markings – though the word "normal" was dropped from the revised colour standards; published by the Budgerigar Society in 1994.

Bill and Chris Heale:

In our eyes, a good Spangle needs first to be a good exhibition Budgerigar in its own right. In addition, it must display distinct wing markings, rich, even body colour, have bulls-eye mask spots and it should also be a Normal. Although we breed Opaline Spangles, we do not like them. Based on show results and what we have observed while stewarding, we do not believe that double-factor Spangles stand a chance against Normal Spangles and Opaline Spangles. A bad Budgerigar is one that has such faults as poor deportment, lacking head width, hinged tail, beakiness, crossed flights and shallow mask. Even if a Budgerigar is otherwise a good specimen, as far as we are concerned, it is a bad Spangle if it is very badly marked, has no spots or has had its markings diluted or masked by being combined with another mutation such as Dominant Pied, Recessive Pied, Lutino, Albino or Clearwing.

Reinhard Molkentin:

A good Spangle must be a good exhibition Budgerigar with the added feature of good Spangle markings. That means that the wing of a Spangle Light Green should be clear yellow with a hem of distinct black near the edge of each feather. Likewise, the wing of a Spangle Skyblue should be clear white with a hem of distinct black near the edge of each feather. The mask spots on Spangles are so distinctive that they have to be considered an important aspect of the variety. No other mutation has the feature of a clear area in the centre of a black surrounding spot. The black spot itself, in size and shape, should conform with that of a good Normal. A Spangle which is considered bad because of its markings would have washed out markings on the wings, wings with a body colour overwash and spots that are ill-defined, invisible or solid black.

Which faults are correctable and which are not?

Jeff Attwood:

From the point of view of a particular variety, there is no fault that cannot be corrected – as long as there are enough features of the original variety available. The Budgerigar Society Colour Standards Committee must accept its share of the blame for not setting standards that, first and foremost, maintain the characteristics of the original mutations. Fortunately, there are still one or two purists who maintain the original Spangle markings and so the means exist to correct Spangle marking faults. There is, perhaps, one exception to the principle I have just stated and that involves wing markings, mainly on cocks, that fade as the bird ages. We cannot change the aging process. To be more specific, if you have Spangles which are lacking in wing markings, go out and find a stud in which the majority of Spangles are well marked. Acquire a Spangle from this stud – it does not matter if it is not a good exhibition specimen – and start working with it to improve your own Spangles' markings. For both wing markings and body colour, it is best to avoid mutations such as Cinnamon and Opaline and washed-out colours, like Grey Green. The Dark factor always gives good colour contrast. Spangles' spots are a problem as, in my experience, they are quite unpredictable. Spangles with good spots produce young with no spots at all – and vice versa. For this reason, I believe that spots on Spangles should not be given the same importance as on the Normal varieties. It would be far better to follow the example of the Recessive Pied standard and accept that there need not be any mask spots at all.

Vic Smith:

Most Budgerigar faults can be corrected. The exceptions are nipped-in neck and hinged tail. Any Budgerigar displaying either of those faults has no place in my stud. Correcting and avoiding faults is all about

A super Spangle Grey Green cock that lacks spots, but is still a valuable Budgerigar.

careful selection of pairings. There are two general rules, 1) you should never pair two Budgerigars together that have the same fault and 2) if a bird needs to be improved in some respect you need to find a mate that excels in the required feature. Observing those two rules should result in the breeding of balanced Budgerigars.

Bill and Chris Heale:

As far as the Budgerigar itself is concerned, it is very difficult to eradicate the faults of lack of head width, beakiness and hinged tail and we would not use Budgerigars with these faults in our breeding programme. Depth of mask can be corrected and it is possible to vary feather texture - more buff feathering or finer, yellow feathering - by pairing correctly. Markings on Spangles can be improved by pairing with quality Normals. A particular problem of the Spangle variety is that their spots can vary from one moult to the next. A Spangle with good spots can moult new ones which are not so good.

Reinhard Molkentin:

As I have already stated, the difference between a good and a bad Spangle - as an example of its variety - lies in the definition of its markings. If a Spangle is poorly marked, improvement can be brought about by pairing Spangle to Spangle. This very similar to the best way of improving the clarity of wings of Clearwings; pair Clearwing with Clearwing. One of the worst possible combinations is Spangle Opaline Cinnamon, the definition of markings is so diluted that it is often impossible to tell what the genetic make-up of the bird is. Many are so pale, they resemble Dilutes. If you are interested in preserving the beauty of Spangles, never cross them with Opaline Cinnamons!

What do you see as being the strength of your own stud? What do you think of other breeders' and other countries' Spangles?

Jeff Attwood:

A strength of my Spangle stud is that I have a relatively large number of the variety - including many with true Spangle characteristics. This has not happened by chance. I am dedicated to retaining the true characteristics of all of the varieties I keep. For example, while developing the American Clearbody I found that as soon as I increased their size they lost their distinctive markings. I now retain well-marked examples even if they are poor exhibition Budgerigars. I realise that I will need to progress more slowly. As far as Spangles are concerned, I have a large number of Budgerigars that are ideal as mates for them; Dark factors (including Violets) and Australian Goldenfaces. I would like to produce a greater proportion of Spangles that combine being excellent Budgerigars with the correct markings, but even the best studs do well to produce more than one top-class winner from every 50 Budgerigars bred. Though there are German breeders who seem to be able to better that average. From the many studs I have seen the world over, there are numerous fanciers I admire. With one exception, I will name only British studs. The exception is Germany's Jo Mannes whose stud is outstanding. In the UK I may be biased, but I was totally appreciative of Mrs Moss's stud. I would have loved to have seen what that lady would have made of Spangles when she was in her heyday; the 1950s, 60s and early-70s. She was one of the greatest. In my 40 years in the Fancy I've seen them come and I've seen them go – and the best breeders were not always the best exhibitors. The studs of Alf Ormerod, Tom Rothery and George Jenkins were outstanding in their day. Harry Bryan, Alf Ormerod and Mrs Moss had the ability to bring Budgerigars together that produced outstanding progeny, time after time. Other names that come to mind are: Jim Moffat – consistently good Budgerigars with lovely faces, shoulders and heads; Chris Snell and his late father, Arthur – progressed through the Fancy at the same time as me but were more successful; Brian Byles – super, solid birds with great head qualities and lovely, long feathering, perhaps the last true "Finey" bloodline; Rodney Harris – has wonderful Budgerigars, though he tends to keep to the west of England he would hold his own anywhere. As far as other countries are concerned: good Spangles are not as widespread in the USA as in Europe; there are some well-marked Spangles in Australia (the fanciers there tend to take more notice of slight differences in marking) but the overall quality of their Budgerigars is not yet as good as those in the UK. In general, only German Spangles have anything to offer to those in the UK. When I judged the BS Club Show, a couple of years ago, I did not see a Spangle to compare with the Spangle Dark Green cock exhibited by Vic Smith in 1984.

Vic Smith:

At the time of writing, my stud is strongest in Cinnamons and Opaline Cinnamons. There are a number of features that I would like to improve, but a fact that works against achieving lasting improvements is that many present-day Budgerigars do not live long enough for a plan to be fully put into action. This may well be our fault. The reduction in their longevity may well have been brought about by the craze for size in our exhibition birds. In years gone by (I just hate to mention how many!) I had cock Budgerigars, which were dominant for good points and which would still be producing chicks at the age of six or seven years. You could breed back to such a bird to reinforce the good points that you had established.

That sort of line-breeding is no longer possible. Although I do not wish to name names, I can state that I admire a number of today's fanciers. What I DO know is that no single person dominates the Budgerigar Fancy in Britain today – and that is a good thing. The quality of the Spangles I saw in Germany, bred by Reinhard Molkentin, back in December 1983 was outstanding. Whether German Spangles are still as good I cannot say, but the Spangles I now see in Britain could not have lived with those bred by Harry Bryan, Doug Sadler, Alf Ormerod and Jeff Attwood in the early days.

Bill and Chris Heale:

We believe the strength of our own Spangles lies in their broad shoulders, depth of mask, style and wing markings. We would still like to improve their bulls-eye spots. In general, we have been working to get a little more feather on our birds without getting too buff. So far we are extremely pleased with the results of our efforts. We see Budgerigars differently. Bill prefers the "blowey-headed" Budgerigars favoured in the south of England, whereas Chris likes the cap-headed, buffier birds that are more popular in the north. We keep both types. The number of well-marked Spangles seen on the show bench has dwindled recently. Many show uneven

A Spangle Grey cock from the Bill & Chris Heale birdroom.

and blotchy wing markings with body colour evident on the wings. Some have solid spots or no spots at all. Double-factor Spangles are tending to show too much uneven tinging (blue on white or green on yellow). The size of Spangles compares very well with other varieties. We cannot single out individual breeders for the excellence of their Spangle lines, because each aviary has its own particular features that we like. If they could all be put together you would have the right mix for an outstanding exhibition Spangle. Having said that, a few years ago Doug Sadler had some very good, well-marked Spangles which we admired. Eric Crouch also bred one or two very well-marked Spangles. We both admired Amos & Thumwood's Spangle that was best Spangle at the Specialist & Rare Variety Budgerigar show in 1992. Patsy and Bruce Harper have bred several well-marked examples and, although we only saw it in photographs, Joe Nevin's Spangle that took the young bird CC at Budgerigar World show looked very good. It appears, from photographs, that some of the German-bred Spangles have lovely markings and true bulls-eye spots.

Reinhard Molkentin:

The strength of any stud lies in the quality of the bloodlines on which it was based. All of my Budgerigars go back to the bloodlines of Alf Ormerod, Doug Sadler and Mrs Angela Moss. Recently, I have paired my old stud with Germany's most successful Budgerigars and my results are approaching their very best, in terms of both quality and quantity. In 1991 and 1992 I brought together all the necessary qualities in my stud so that I would have 250 Budgerigars to take with me to South Africa. In the first five years in the new country I will be establishing my stud and be preparing to exhibit in competition. I admire fanciers who put a lot of effort into working with and developing their studs of Budgerigars, also those who think up new ideas and approaches – and pursue them. When it comes to the Budgerigars themselves, I admire a beautiful specimen no matter who bred it. Spangles, because of their popularity, improved at a tremendous rate. Indeed, based on my knowledge of the Spangle in Europe, I can say that the only variety to come anywhere near its speed of improvement was the Dominant Pied. When I think back to the original Australian-bred Spangles that I first saw, it is almost like a dream to see what has resulted from them. The length of the Australian Spangles was at most 200mm (8.0in). The width of their heads was between 16 and 16.5mm (0.6 – 0.65in). Spangles are now the size of the best Normals at more than 240mm (9.5in) and their head width is no different to Normals and Opalines at between 18 and 20mm (0.7 – 0.8in). As far as feather quality is concerned, we have already transferred everything to the Spangle that is required.

What is the best way of breeding a good Spangle?

Jeff Attwood:

To breed good Spangles you need to use Budgerigars that not only display good Spangle characteristics but have also been bred from stock that is outstanding in those characteristics. These birds, when identified, need to paired in such a way as to balance their markings with the overall quality required of an exhibition Budgerigar of any variety. I see no reason why single-factor Spangle to single-factor Spangle matings should not be used – as long as both are well-marked. The double-factor Spangles and Normals produced from this sort of mating can be very useful in the future production of single-factor Spangles. Double-factor Spangle to single-factor Spangle and double-factor Spangle to Normal are both pairings that have produced good single-factor Spangles for me. When I pair Normals with Spangles I prefer them to be single Dark factors; Dark Greens, Cobalts and Violets. The Australian Goldenface mutation displays Spangle markings to excellent effect. With one exception, I have avoided pairing Opalines with Spangles. The exception was when I used an Opaline hen to improve head, shoulder and mask qualities. I was careful to use Normals in the next generation. I see no point whatsoever in pairing Spangles with Cinnamons, Albinos, Lutinos or Recessive Pieds.

I am a great believer in inbreeding. It started by accident. A cock and a hen I acquired from Mrs Moss happened to be first-cousins and, not knowing this, I paired them together and produced outstanding youngsters. Since then I have found cousin x cousin to be one of the finest matings. I have also used father x daughter, mother x son and half-brother x half-sister with some success. I very rarely use grandparent x grandchild pairings and, although I have tried brother x sister pairings, nothing good ever came of them. The important thing about making pairings as closely-related as this is that the birds need to be of excellent quality to start with. I would never recommend a newcomer to use inbreeding. If I obtained an outstanding, unrelated cock, I would pair it with the best complementary hen I could spare and pair its best daughter back to it the following year. However, if inbreeding is a quick road to success, it can also be a quick road to disaster – even in the hands of experienced breeders. The problem is, that even though you are careful to start with very fertile stock, fertility reduces as years pass and you can be getting all clear eggs as soon as four years after starting an inbreeding programme. So it is advisable to bring in an outcross every three years. One approach is to start two line-bred families at the same time and to cross a bird from one line into the other when required. My Cinnamons are an example of an inbred family that has kept going. It produced its first winners in 1970 and continues to do so up to the present day. My best breeder at the 1988 Budgerigar Society Club Show was from this line.

Vic Smith:

Assuming that you know how to breed a Budgerigar of reasonable quality, I can move straight on to the points that are special to the Spangle. Wing markings are very important. Some of the Spangles you see are too lightly laced, while others are too heavily marked. If you pair a lightly-marked Spangle with a heavily-marked Spangle, a number of the single-factor Spangle chicks that are produced should have the correct level of lacing. Because Spangle Opalines are so often very lightly marked I would never consider pairing two Spangle Opalines together. When it comes to relationships, I have never bred closer than half-brother to half-sister and that was an excellent pairing.

Bill and Chris Heale:

We can speak from experience here. Bill won our first Spangle Opaline Grey Green cock in a judging contest and we paired it with our best Normal Green hen. The young cocks we produced were paired with the Green hen's sisters. The Normals produced were line-bred back to the Spangles. We have found that if a completely different bloodline is used, the wing markings come out uneven and show body colour. As long as we line-breed, the markings are well defined and other good features are maintained. We are prepared to pair Spangle with Spangle, to produce double-factors, as long as they are both of good quality. The double-factors are then paired with Normals to produce 100 per cent Spangles to provide stock for future breeding programmes. Spangles paired with Normals that have been bred from Spangles produce well-defined wing markings. We do not pair mother to son, father to daughter or brother to sister. However, we have enjoyed good results from grandfather x grand-daughter, grandmother x grandson, aunt x nephew, uncle x niece and half-sister x half-brother pairings. By line-breeding we maintain certain features. We took the best beginner breeder award at South Hampshire championship show in 1985 with an Opaline Grey hen and the same family is still producing winners.

Reinhard Molkentin:

No matter what variety I am setting out to breed, my overriding consideration is always to breed a good Budgerigar. Having said that, some pairings produce better-marked Spangles than others. My favourite pairings are Spangle x Spangle and double-factor Spangle x Normal. In my stud, these have produced the best markings. I have also bred good Spangles from Spangle x Normal, Spangle x Opaline and Spangle x Cinnamon – with Spangle x Normal being the preferred mating of the three. As far as relationships are concerned, I have tried them all; inbreeding, line-breeding, distant relatives and unrelated stock. My conclusion is that line-breeding –

cousin x cousin, uncle x niece, aunt x nephew and similar – is the best. I believe that breeding closer than that brings problems. In any case, with all of the bloodlines that exist in the world there is no need to pair so close.

How would you advise a newcomer to Spangles to set up a successful stud?

Jeff Attwood:

Before you try to set up a stud of Spangles you should first set out to understand the variety. You should get to know an experienced breeder and ask questions so that you can learn from his mistakes. Then, I would advise obtaining a minimum of two pairs, each made up of a single-factor Spangle and a Normal; from a breeder who has made a name for winning with his own-bred Spangles. The Normals should have been bred from his Spangles and, ideally will be Dark-factor birds so that you have good contrast from the start. After the first breeding season, do not let any youngsters go until they have moulted out. Then keep all Normals that display reasonable quality, Spangles that have distinct markings and Spangles that are particularly good Budgerigars, even if their markings are not good. For the second breeding season, pair the chicks from the original pairings. Depending on what progress you make, you may find it necessary to go back and buy another bird – possibly an older cock of better quality than the originals. Take two or three of your best chicks with you and you may even be able to arrange an exchange. Around the third year it will be advisable to bring in a complete outcross – not necessarily a Spangle – to avoid infertility.

Vic Smith:

As a newcomer, you should visit as many shows as possible, study the young bird classes and purchase birds from a fancier who is successful in these classes. I would recommend buying two young pairs; Spangle cocks and Normal hens. For preference, the Spangles will also be Normals and – to show the markings to best effect – carrying a Dark-factor; Dark Green or Cobalt. Opaline Spangles should be avoided because their wings tend to be smudgy in appearance; devoid of the desirable lacings. If you have a reasonable first breeding season you should have a number of useful Spangles to get you off to a good start as a beginner on the show bench and as breeding stock for your second year. I would then advise going back to the original fancier to buy a couple of birds of better quality. If your first breeding season was REALLY successful you may even be able to arrange an exchange of birds.

Bill and Chris Heale:

If you have no experience of livestock, you would be best advised to breed brightly-coloured Budgerigars for a couple of years to get an idea of what is involved. The pretty chicks that are bred will be easier to sell as pets, to help pay for seed. During the two years, you should join a cage bird or Budgerigar society, go to shows, join in aviary visits and, if possible, get out of your area as much as possible. You should know, after that, whether you still want to keep exhibition Budgerigars. If so, still keep a few pairs of pets to act as foster-parents for your new stock. We think you need at least 10 pairs to generate enough activity to encourage breeding. Check who is winning in the young bird classes at the big shows. They do not have to be champions as many challenge certificates go to the lower sections these days. The aim should be to buy the lesser relatives from the best bloodlines; five pairs from each of two studs that have related stock. There is every chance that the first breeding season will produce useful Budgerigars. A helpful, experienced fancier will let you have more related birds for the second breeding season. We are great believers in bloodlines. No matter what form of livestock you consider – cats, dogs, horses or cattle – the best stock comes from related bloodlines. Once you are established, it is up to you to decide whether to stay with the same line or whether to start buying from new sources which will dilute the pedigree of the birds.

Reinhard Molkentin:

I would advise purchasing three pairs from a reputable breeder. Choose three Normals and three Normal Spangles. It does not matter what colour they are. With average luck you will breed enough to give a reasonable choice of pairings the following year. Youngster to youngster and youngster to adult matings can be made – avoiding brother to sister and parent to offspring. If the theoretical expectations work out in practice you should have roughly equal numbers of Spangles and non-Spangles. It is worth considering Spangle x Spangle pairings as I have found these to produce good markings. You will probably also produce double-factor Spangles, which I have found to be very useful, as when paired with Normals they produce all single-factor Spangles.

How important is it for you to ring chicks at the earliest possible time?

Jeff Attwood:

If you really want to have chicks ready for ringing when the Budgerigar Society official rings arrive, at the beginning of January, you need to pair up during the third week in November – which is completely the wrong time as far as the birds are concerned. The turn of the year, when days are shortest and the weather is cold is NOT the best time to have chicks in the nest. I have found that the end of September is the best time to pair Budgerigars; just as they come out of the moult. This is when they are fighting fit. The days are still long and temperatures are still quite high and – most important – it coincides with the spring season in Australia. In spite of being domesticated for so long, Budgerigars still have the instinct to go to nest at that time. If the conventional time to pair Budgerigars was September there would be many more of them bred – especially from the better birds. Alternatively, late February, when the the days are lengthening and temperatures are rising, is another good time to pair Budgerigars.

Vic Smith:

Although I prefer the breeding season to the show season I am never in any hurry to get started. The main thing is to pair up when the birds are fit. For the last few years I have not paired up my Budgerigars until mid-January and they have bred very well. I do not worry about trying to get chicks in the nest-boxes for when the rings arrive.

Bill and Chris Heale:

It is reasonably important to ring chicks early in the year though, having said that, our best show birds usually come from the second and third breeding rounds; mainly hatched in mid-February through to March. Our main aim is to pair when the birds are in breeding condition. We have put up pairs in early October because they were raring to go. This paid off in the number of chicks produced. As long as we keep the numbers of particular families at the level we require, it is unimportant what colour rings they are wearing.

Reinhard Molkentin:

In Germany, official rings are issued on October 1, but it does not matter whether a good chick has this year's or last year's ring. When a hen definitely wants to breed, that is the time I pair her up. I am sure that my breeding results have benefited from this approach. The time of the year that rings are sent out has no effect on me.

How do you go about acquiring stock of the required quality?

Jeff Attwood:

Although it would be nice to introduce a Budgerigar of outstanding quality, there is not much prospect these days. And if one does come onto the market it tends to be quite old. I have not bought many birds from UK breeders in recent years. I prefer to let very good birds go to breeders I know and trust and then get a chick back off them; the product of my own bloodline and the best of theirs. I call this an "incross/outcross". If I ever bring in an outstanding, unrelated bird it is either by way of swapping in the UK or purchasing from abroad.

Vic Smith:

The only way to get a good, outcross (preferably unrelated) is to be prepared to let a very good Budgerigar go in exchange.

Bill and Chris Heale:

For the past few years we have found exchanging birds to be the best policy.

This young Spangle Skyblue cock would be an ideal outcross.

Reinhard Molkentin:

I like to keep my bloodlines pure, so it makes no sense to pair unrelated stock with my Spangles.

Do you ever sell the best Spangles from your stud?

Jeff Attwood:

If I breed a large number of good birds I can afford to part with a few of the better ones, though I do not sell top-line birds until I have had one or two breeding seasons from them. I advise newcomers to avoid selling their best birds to champions, even if it is for an apparently good price. You can be sure that the champion would have to pay more for a Budgerigar of equivalent quality if he was buying it from another champion.

Vic Smith:

I never sell my best Budgerigars. I am in the hobby because I like breeding and studying Budgerigars and so money would never tempt me to sell a bird I want to keep. I sell only the birds I want to sell.

Bill and Chris Heale:

We do not sell our best Spangles. It is very difficult to breed "super" birds. They appear only a few times in a lifetime. Where could you buy a Budgerigar of equal quality? Nowhere! There is no reason why lesser relatives should not produce a "super" bird, as long as they are line-bred.

Reinhard Molkentin:

No. The best Spangles always stay in the stud. Otherwise, the standard of the variety would decrease.

What, in your opinion, is the degree of difficulty of Spangles?

Jeff Attwood:

I have no doubt that Spangles are a more difficult variety than Normals or Opalines. A true Spangle needs super wing markings combined with all of the good points that go to make a good exhibition specimen. One of the most difficult aspects of the Spangle is its spots. I have found that these are inherited in a random fashion and believe that allowance should be made for this in the standard.

Vic Smith:

Spangles are no more difficult to breed to high standards than any other dominant Budgerigar variety. The difficulty lies in getting the correct wing lacing and mask spots with clear centres.

Bill and Chris Heale:

Spangles are difficult in so far as it is not easy to maintain well-defined markings, bulls-eye spots and size, all on the same bird.

Reinhard Molkentin:

Over and above the difficulties associated with other varieties, you must get the correct markings on a Spangle. The markings on the wings and flights need to be correct and also the mask spots. Each spot should consist of a two crescent-shaped dark markings which touch at top and bottom, with a light centre in between.

Even Spangles can produce the odd feather-duster for Reinhard Molkentin.

Are there any tactics that can help you win with Spangles?
Jeff Attwood:

You can never make a mediocre Budgerigar into a great one but, merely by show preparation, you CAN make it into a good one. When I exhibited a lot I used to get annoyed to hear some exhibitors complaining that a certain few were winning every week. Many of the complaints came from people who caught their birds out of the flight on the morning of the show. Quite often, you could see the labels from previous shows still on their cages. No matter how well I prepared a bird I always felt that if I had been allowed another day, I could have done it better. That is the attitude that leads to success. Overshowing can affect a Budgerigar's chances. For each bird, I like there to be two or three weeks between each show and preferably no more than three shows in a season. It helps if you get to know the judges, as most have particular preferences. Then you can find a bird that will please the judge. If you don't know the judge, it pays to put two or three in each class – of different types.

Vic Smith:

If you have a good Spangle – or any other variety of Budgerigar for that matter – if it is going to stand any chance of winning you must prepare it properly and stage it to best advantage. A nice, clean show cage makes a difference. When I am judging, I cannot help noticing a well-presented cage – even though I am always aware that it is the birds I am assessing. I have known a good show cage to make the difference between first and second place, when two birds were of equal merit. Some judges favour one colour above another, so I try to enter a range of colours – various shades of Blue, Green and Grey – in the same class so that the judge can take his choice.

Bill and Chris Heale:

Show preparation! That's what makes a good Budgerigar a winner. We have seen countless Budgerigars, over the years, that could have been major winners if only their owners had prepared them properly. When we were first-year novices we took notice of Bristol champion, Margaret Dark, when she advised us to wash our Budgerigars' heads, especially above their ceres where they so often look grubby. It has certainly worked for us. Exhibitors should also make sure that their show cages are in good condition. There is nothing worse than seeing an excellent Budgerigar in a tatty cage. Our show cages are repainted every year. We normally show no more than two birds in a class at major shows. We are more interested in young birds than adults so tend to show more in young bird classes.

Reinhard Molkentin:

As with all other varieties, you need a good Budgerigar that has been well prepared if you are to stand a chance of winning. As I have stressed previously, a Spangle's markings are extremely important and there is not a great deal that you can do if the bird does not have good markings to start with. However, I can offer one tip regarding spots. Some Spangles appear to have undesirable, solid spots but when you lift these you find proper Spangle spots beneath. Removing the solid spots can make a difference to Spangle's chances on the show bench. When exhibiting I do not find it necessary to enter more than two Spangle in each class. I always enter my best two – as long as they are fit.

Reinhard Molkentin gives a couple of young Spangles some show cage training.

How do you go about judging Spangles?

Jeff Attwood:

I believe it is important that a judge is seen to study every bird entered; even if a class contains 50 exhibits. I look for birds with major faults – both tail feathers, several flights or more than one spot missing, a head full of quill feathers, terribly out of condition, the cere the wrong colour – and eliminate them from the judging trestle, so leaving the real contenders. Typical show faults – such as a dropped tail – are penalised, as with any other variety. I would only disqualify a bird if it was not a Spangle. As a specialist breeder, I am very aware of the importance of wing markings when judging Spangles. I understand the problem of Spangle spots and so do not penalise the lack of them as severely as some other judges. I look for a good contrast between wings and body so Dark Greens and Cobalts catch my eye more than Greys and Grey Greens. I can see that there is some justification in asking for specialist judges for varieties like Clearwings and Lutinos, but I do not see Spangles as being in that category. In any case, judges should at least study – if not keep – the varieties they are judging. All the combinations of Spangle being in the same class is not helpful to judges, because once mutations like Cinnamon and Opaline are involved, the wing markings are devalued. I also believe the double-factor Spangle should be treated as a variety in its own right. When they were in the Any Other Colour class it was unfair to some recessive varieties but putting them in with single-factor Spangles has put double-factor Spangles at a disadvantage.

Jeff Attwood believes that double-factor Spangles are put at a disadvantage when shown in the same class as single-factor Spangles.

Vic Smith:

Judging Spangles is no different to judging any other variety of Budgerigar. I start by looking along the class to assess the overall quality. I then proceed to eliminate any inferior specimens. If it is a big class, I retain about 10 exhibits on the judging trestle. I then place the birds in order until I have eliminated the last three. As far as I am concerned, a Budgerigar Society panel judge should be capable of judging any variety; from Grey Greens through Recessive Pieds and Whitewings and right on to Crests. Being human, some judges are better than others so, over a period of time, you win some and lose some. However, I am prepared to bench my Budgerigars under any BS panel judge.

Bill and Chris Heale:

To win, a Spangle would have to be a good exhibition Budgerigar, displaying distinct markings, bulls-eye spots and even body colour. A Double-factor Spangle's body colour should be quite even with not too many tinges of green or blue. Lack of distinct markings, lack of spots, uneven wing markings, body colour on the wings and the physical faults associated with all varieties should disqualify an exhibit from winning. We exhibit under judges who do not specialise in Spangles but are not very happy about it. We believe that judges should breed and exhibit the varieties they judge – otherwise they cannot know what to look for. We both steward at open shows and have heard one judge ask another what he should be looking for when judging Spangles. The recent revision of Colour Standards has given more points for markings and is an improvement on what went before. We are not happy about double-factor Spangles having to compete with single-factors as we feel that this could result in breeders losing interest in the double-factor form which, used wisely, can help the development of a Spangle stud.

Reinhard Molkentin:

When judging Spangles I look first for type, then for markings and, finally, for head quality and mask. I fault Spangles for all of the same reasons as any other variety. In addition, if a Spangle lacks melanin, it stands no chance of winning. I believe that there are certain varieties (such as Recessive Pieds and Clearwings) which are best judged by specially chosen judges who have experience of the variety concerned. In my opinion, Spangles come into the same category. As far as Ideal standards are concerned, I have no problems with the ones laid down by any of the administering bodies.

How do you see the future of Spangles?
Jeff Attwood:

I fear that unless we get some forward-looking people setting the standards, we will see the Spangle decline in the same way that Opalines and Clearwings have done. As a pessimist, I can envisage the future continuing to be dominated by Normal Grey Greens, but the good news is that another Spangle mutation has appeared in Brisbane, Australia. When I went there I located it in several birdrooms, so it is already well established. It is different from the original Spangle in that in nest feather plumage it looks just like a Normal, except for a clear tail. When it moults it evolves into a recognisable Spangle, except that it has full, black spots and the cheek patch is unbroken violet. In every case, the wing marking remain quite distinct. The examples I saw were Greens and it appears that the body colour has also mutated into a shade between Light and Dark Green. They had a lovely, solid apple-green coloration. I have recently seen a few "Brisbane" Spangles on the British show bench, in the north and midlands. My hope for the distant future is that in 50 years time, Budgerigar breeders will be able to appreciate the true beauty of the Spangle; just as it was when they were first brought from Australia in the 1970s.

Vic Smith:

I live in hope that, over the next 10 years the Spangle variety will make better progress than it has over the last decade. I can assure you that I will be doing my best to rectify the situation.

Bill and Chris Heale:

The future of Spangles depends upon three factors: the colour standards reflecting the specific points of the variety; breeders not pairing them with varieties that dilute the markings and extra classes being provided so that Opaline and other variety Spangles do not have to compete with Normal Spangles. Unless things change, we see Spangles going the same way as Dominant Pieds and Yellowfaces, with the numbers exhibited declining. The future lies in the hands of the administrators but, for ourselves, we will continue to strive to breed Spangles with good markings.

Reinhard Molkentin:

Unlike Recessive Pieds and Clearwings, Spangles are no longer regarded as "colour birds". Spangles are fully integrated into the studs of the world's best Budgerigar breeders and have had a positive effect on their Normals. I am now breeding better Normals, Cinnamons and Opalines than ever before – and all of them have Spangles in their pedigrees. I firmly believe that Spangles have a great future.

CHAPTER 7

COLOUR EXPECTATIONS

The subject of Budgerigar colour expectations could fill a book on its own – in fact it HAS filled a book and anyone who wants to delve deeper into the subject should read Taylor and Warner's *Genetics for Budgerigar Breeders*.

Understanding genetics CAN help when it comes to breeding good Budgerigars, but it must be stressed that many of the breeders who have bred the best Budgerigars in the world have had only a sketchy knowledge of the subject. So, if you find the subject difficult to understand you will be in good company, and should not worry unduly. However, if you have ever been surprised by the appearance of a Normal in the nest of two Spangles, or how a Blue turns up in the nest of two Greens, read on!

The first fact that needs to be understood is that, in every case, there are TWO factors controlling every individual colour and variety. In this book, the letters used to denote these are not necessarily the ones that are used in serious text books. For the sake of the first example, a Spangle factor is represented by the letter "S" and a non-Spangle factor by "N". So double-factor Spangle (DF) is "SS", a single-factor Spangle (SF) is "SN" and any Budgerigar with no Spangle factor is "NN". When two Budgerigars mate, each gives ONE of its colour factors to each chick. The possible combinations can be represented by a grid of four squares. So what happens when two single-factor Spangle Budgerigars mate and each parent passes on one of its factors to each chick?

Spangle (SF)

	S	N
S	SS	SN
N	SN	NN

Spangle (SF)

A quarter of the chicks will be "SS" (double-factor Spangles), a half will be "SN" (single-factor Spangles) and a quarter will be "NN" (non-Spangles). Because Spangle is dominant to non-Spangle, a Budgerigar possessing only one Spangle factor will still look like a Spangle. A characteristic of the variety is that the double-factor form (being virtually a "Clear" bird) looks quite different to the single-factor. This is markedly different to another dominant form; the Grey. Double and single-factor Greys are indistinguishable visually and it is only by test-mating that their genetic make-up can be established.

The following grid demonstrates what happens when a single-factor Spangle ("SN") is paired with a non-Spangle ("NN"):

Spangle (SF)

		S	N
non-Spangle	N	SN	NN
	N	SN	NN

Half of the chicks will be "SN" (single-factor Spangles) and the rest will be "NN" (non-Spangles).

Next, let us check an "NS" (single-factor Spangle) x "SS" (double-factor Spangle) mating.

Spangle (SF)

		S	N
Spangle (DF)	S	SS	SN
	S	SS	SN

All of the chicks will be Spangle, equally divided between double and single-factor.

The same procedure will show that a double factor Spangle x double-factor Spangle mating will produce all double-factor Spangles, two non-Spangles paired together will produce all non-Spangles and a double-factor Spangle paired with a non-Spangle will produce all single-factor Spangles.

In the same way that Spangle is dominant to non-Spangle, Green is dominant to Blue. If a Green factor is denoted by "G" and a Blue factor by "B" then a Green is "GG" and a Blue is "BB". A Budgerigar that carries one Green and one Blue factor "GB" is known as a Green split Blue (Green/Blue) and, visually, is no different to a Green "GG". The outcome of pairing two Green/Blues ("GB") together follows the same pattern as pairing two single-factor Spangles.

Green split Blue

	G	B
G	GG	GB
B	GB	BB

Green Split Blue

A quarter of the chicks will be "GG" (Greens), a half will be "GB" (Green split Blue, like their parents) and a quarter will be "BB" – Blues! That is how Blue Budgerigars can be bred from two that look just like Greens.

As long as you remember that a Spangle Green is a Green with a Spangle factor added and a Spangle Blue is a Blue with a Spangle factor added it is fairly easy to work out, in two stages, the outcome of all the pairing combinations of Spangles, non-Spangles, Greens and Blues.

If you wish to read how the Dark factor works to produce Cobalts, Violets, Mauves, Dark Greens and Olives, you will find an explanation in other books in this series (eg *All About Green Budgerigars* and *All About Blue Budgerigars*). But the adventurous may wish to carry out their own investigation by denoting Lights a "LL", Medium as "LD" and Dark as "DD".

For those who have no wish to calculate colour expectations, the following tables will prove useful.

TABLE 1: Pairings involving Spangles and non-Spangles
(with theoretical percentage expectations)

Pairing*	Expectations (cocks and hens)
Spangle (DF) × Spangle (DF)	100% Spangle (DF)
Spangle (DF) × Spangle (SF)	50% Spangle (DF) 50% Spangle (SF)
Spangle (DF) × non-Spangle	100% Spangle (SF)
Spangle (SF) × Spangle (SF)	25% Spangle (DF) 50% Spangle (SF) 25% non-Spangle
Spangle (SF) × non-Spangle	50% Spangle (SF) 50% non-Spangle
non-Spangle × non-Spangle	100% non-Spangle

* *(It makes no difference which colour is the cock and which is the hen)*

TABLE 2: Pairings involving Greens and Blues
(with theoretical percentage expectations)

Pairing*	Expectations (cocks and hens)
Green × Green	100% Green
Green × Blue	100% Green/Blue
Green × Green/Blue	50% Green 50% Green/Blue
Green/Blue × Green/Blue	25% Green 50% Green/Blue 25% Blue
Green/Blue × Blue	50% Green/Blue 50% Blue
Blue × Blue	100% Blue

* *(It makes no difference which colour is the cock and which is the hen)*

TABLE 3: Pairings involving Light Greens, Dark Greens and Olives.
(with theoretical percentage expectations)

Pairing*	Expectations (cocks and hens)
Light Green × Light Green	100% Light Green
Light Green × Dark Green	50% Light Green 50% Dark Green
Light Green × Olive	100% Dark Green
Dark Green × Dark Green	25% Light Green 50% Dark Green 25% Olive
Dark Green × Olive	50% Dark Green 50% Olive
Olive × Olive	100% Olive

* *(It makes no difference which colour is the cock and which is the hen)*

Further copies of this book and details about others in the "All about . . ." series can be obtained from:

**F. Wright,
31 Redford Avenue,
Wallington,
Surrey, SM6 9DT
United Kingdom.**

**Telephone or
Fax: 0181-647 6378**

Ask for details of quantity and club discounts

Already in print:
**All about Greens
All about Blues
All about Red-eyes
All about Greys and Grey Greens
All about Spangles
All about Opalines and Opaline
   Cinnamons**
. . . and more are being prepared.

"The Budgerigar Man" The Harry Bryan way of breeding successful exhibition Budgerigars is still available from Fred Wright, at the above address. Price £9.95 plus £2 post and packing (£3 Overseas).

• THE MAGAZINE FOR ALL BREEDERS, KEEPERS AND LOVERS OF BIRDS •

Whether an expert breeder or you are just beginning, Cage & Aviary Birds and Bird keeper magazines are the places to look for tips, advice, news, aviculturist and veterinary features all covered with superb colour photography.

NOW EVERY MONTH £2.00

EVERY THURSDAY ONLY 83p

Available every week or every month from all good newsagents or phone

0444 445533

for details on special money-saving subscriptions.

ipcmagazines